From Ha
Ad

a hundred years of a Sussex family

Deborah Evershed

South Grove Books
Petworth, West Sussex

First Published 2006

© Deborah Evershed 2006

All rights reserved. No reproduction permitted without the prior permission of the publisher:

South Grove Books
3 South Grove
Petworth
West Sussex
GU28 0ED

ISBN 0-9553608-0-3

For my family – past and present

Contents

Preface..5
Introduction..7
Chapter One..9
Chapter Two..25
Chapter Three...43
Chapter Four...65
Chapter Five...79
Chapter Six...95
Chapter Seven..127
Chapter Eight...147
Chapter Nine..173
Epilogue..195

Illustrations

A Map of Adversane in the 1890s..6
Adversane about 1900...78
Alice & Tom's wedding, April 1912.......................................91
Alice & baby Ethel...92
Baby Ethel..93
Evelyn & David Evershed...101
Young Ethel Taylor in the garden at Kingslea.....................123
David & Ethel Evershed's wedding......................................135
Corporal David Evershed...136
The Blacksmith's Arms in the 1950s...................................144
The malthouse cottages in the 1950s..................................145
Frank Sharville & David Evershed dressed for a Victorian
    charity cricket match...169
Fancy dress parade in the early 1950s...............................170
Great grandparents Humphrey...171
Susanna Evershed in her seventies in "Ada".....................178
Antony & Deborah's bonfire fancy dress 1952...................190
Deborah in Coronation costume 1953................................193
Part of Miles family tree...198
Part of Puttock & Taylor family trees..................................199
Part of Evershed family tree..200

Preface

I wrote this book because I wanted to capture a time and a place. It was written originally with my own family in mind, wanting them to know something of the lives of our ancestors in a small but, for us, significant corner of Sussex. Because the book covers a hundred years the vivid memories of my grandparents and elderly relatives provided me with the anecdotes and stories of the early chapters, sometimes given to me at first-hand but more often passed on from them by my parents and aunts. There were times in the past when I thought, "Oh dear. Not this old story again!" Now I fully appreciate what I was being given, and wish I could remember more! The oral tradition includes many small details which often reveal a great deal about people and their everyday lives, as well as recording the major events.

I also wanted to be as historically accurate as possible, so I have spent many hours in the West Sussex Record Office and local libraries, engrossed in maps, censuses and books.

There is one person without whom this would never have happened! I owe a huge debt of gratitude to my husband, Gordon, who has spent countless hours working patiently and uncomplainingly at the computer, preparing the book for publication. His support, technical expertise and practical hard work have been invaluable.

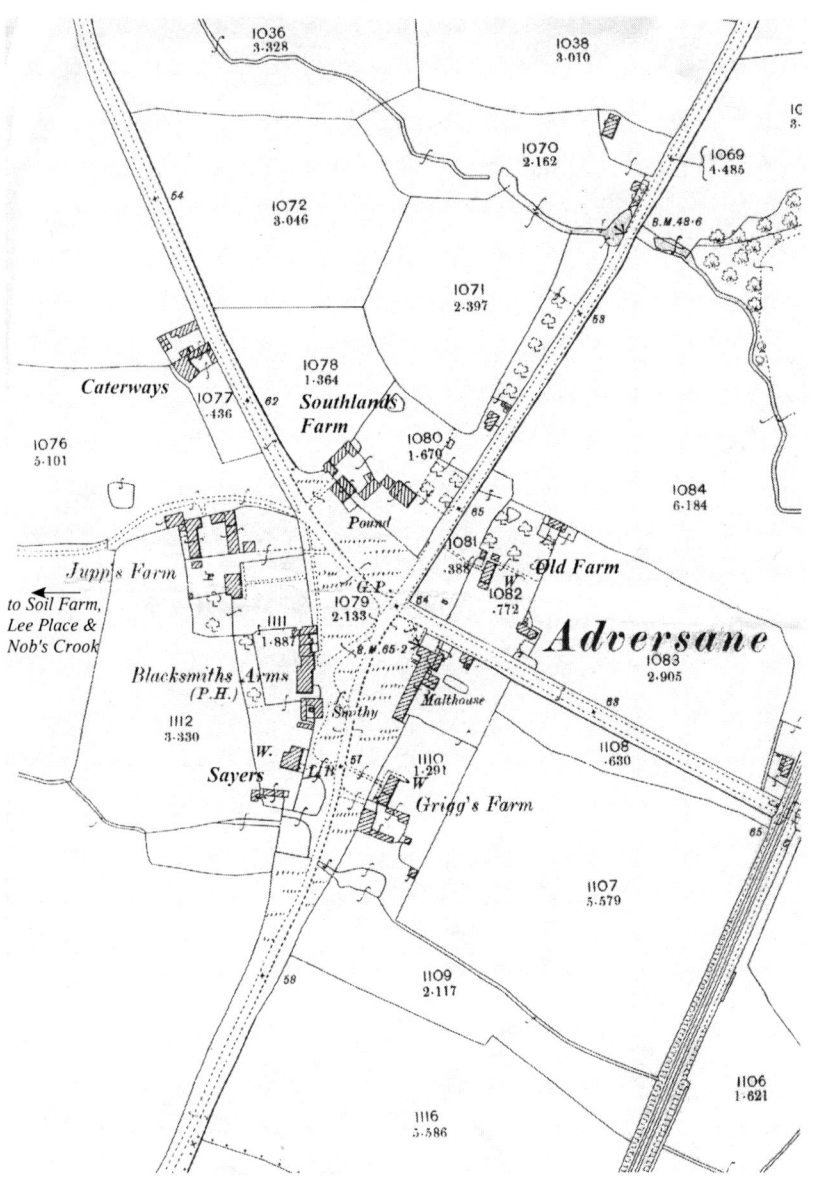

A Map of Adversane in the 1890s

Introduction

By the year of 1856 the ancient West Sussex hamlet of Hadfoldshern had officially become Adversane, although many of the older inhabitants kept to the earlier name. Precisely when and why the change came about is uncertain, but it is likely that someone misunderstood the slow drawl of the Sussex accent and recorded the name incorrectly!

In the mid-19th century the hamlet consisted of a straggle of cottages, dotted round and about a crossroads, several farms, an inn, a smithy and a malthouse. In front of the malthouse there was grassland and a small duck pond. Espalier fruit trees clambered over the mellow sandstone walls of the long, low building, which snuggled under its heavy Horsham stone roof with the air of having grown there quite naturally, like the fruit trees in the gardens behind it.

At the northern end of the malthouse was the maltster's cottage. To the south Richard Stepney's few acres separated the malthouse from Griggs Farm, and adjacent to that stood a fine barn, its solid walls again built from sandstone and its roof of local stone. Beyond the barn a stream meandered into the meadows and filled the pond where Farhall's cattle went to drink and cool off in the hot days of high summer. It was a favourite place with the hamlet children, who walked precariously along the over-hanging willow boughs to peer into the water at the eels which congregated there.

Opposite the barn, on the other side of Stane Street, there was a large duck pond which fed the stream leading into the meadows. This belonged to Sayers, once the property of the late John and Ann Miles, now home to their widowed daughter, Deborah Puttock. With the help of Annie Slater, the only servant, Deborah continued to run the family grocery business in a shop adjacent to the garden. Here she sold drapery as well as groceries, and fresh produce and home-cured bacon produced on her own three acres. Her son, Charles, helped with the heavy outdoor work.

Charles lived next door to Sayers in the Blacksmith's Arms,

with his wife and four children. He was both publican and master blacksmith and worked in the forge, (which was situated between Sayers and the inn), during the day. Dick Harding, his apprentice, also lived in the inn, and young Lizzie Stepney, who helped with the housework.

A grassy common spread to the north of the inn, on either side of the western route into Adversane. To the south of that track were Jupps Farm and Caterways, and between them a narrow lane led to Soil Farm and Lee Place. Southlands Farm, an ancient building even then, was on the northwest corner of the crossroads. A pound stood against its southern wall, from whence the plaintive mooing and bleating of stray beasts was a familiar sound, roaming animals being a common sight.

Miss Baker kept a dame school at the northern edge of the hamlet and helped to make ends meet by giving lodgings to John Gravitt, the hoop-maker. Opposite them was Old Farm and next to that John Harwood's cottage. John was a shoemaker and master craftsman and employed two hands in addition to his own son.

It would take just three more years for the Mid-Sussex Railway to reach Billingshurst, so the winds of change were beginning to blow perilously close to the small community. But in the year of 1856 little had changed in Adversane since it was Hadfoldshern. For the most part, people got on with their lives as their parents and grandparents had done before them: farming, raising their families, using their hands to provide most of what they needed in life. They had to work hard for a living, but there was a peaceful sense of continuity derived from the changing seasons and the demands each one made on them. Over the years there had been some inter-marriage between the families with the result that nearly every household had some connection with all the others. Miles, Puttock, Greenfield, Hard – between these four families there were confusingly tangled threads connecting the generations.

Chapter One

Early in the morning of 25th May 1856 Deborah Puttock was just rising from her bed when there came a frantic banging on the door. She hurried to the window and peered out into the dim daylight.

"Tis me Mother," called Charles. "Mary's in a bad way – can you come?"

"Oh Lord help us – I'll be down d'rectly!"

She got dressed as swiftly as her fingers would allow, and hurried downstairs to the kitchen, where Annie Slater was already stoking the fire.

"Mrs Puttock's time's come, Annie. I'm goin' along now. No – I won't stop for a drink."

Annie watched in dismay as her mistress grabbed up her shawl and stepped smartly out of the door.

"Poor Missus Puttock!" Annie declared to the tabby cat, pouring milk for its breakfast.

It sniffed the milk and sauntered to the door.

Annie let the cat out into the chill morning. She paused a moment, her hand resting on the latch, staring ahead towards the inn. She could just make out its shape as a dark shadow in the early dawn. At first it appeared to be in total darkness, but a small chink of lamplight pierced through the shutters of one of the upstairs windows.

Mrs. Boxall, who helped in the shop, would not be arriving for some time yet. Annie closed the door with a shiver and sat sorrowfully by the range, sipping her tea and thinking how best to help her mistress.

In the Blacksmith's Arms Mary Puttock was in considerable pain. Dick Harding had already left to fetch the doctor from Billingshurst, galloping into the gloom at reckless speed, but it would take some time for the the doctor to get ready and drive his gig to Adversane.

Charles decided the Puttock children should be sent out of

the house to stay with relatives. His mother would be needed to help Mary and the new baby when it was born, so the children could not stay with her. Deborah Puttock came gently into her granddaughter's bedroom, where young Deborah was sitting up in bed, aware of the unusual bustle around the house. The small girl looked nervously at her grandmother.

"What's happening Granny?"

"Father's takin' you and Tommy to stay with Aunt Mary and Uncle Hezekiah for a liddle while my dear, and John and George are goin' to spend a few days with Aunt Sarah."

"Why?" Deborah whined, climbing reluctantly out of the bed.

"Your mother's not well, ducky, so you got to go away, just for a few days, that's all. Now come along and say goodbye to your poor mother. Father's got the horse waitin', so hurry along."

Relieved she would be able to see her mother before she left, Deborah got dressed in record speed, while Grandmother hurriedly pushed some spare clothes into a carpet-bag. Then Deborah was bustled along the passage-way to her parents' room. Grandmother opened the door a crack and peered inside, then said softly,

"Deb's here Mary. Charles is takin' her and Tommy over to Hezekiah's."

Deborah peered fearfully past her grandmother. Mother was lying on the big bed, her eyes screwed up tightly and her face as white as the pillow she rested on. Next to her sat Mrs. Booker, bolt upright on a hard chair. She was the lady who had brought Tommy to live with them. Granny said she carried new babies in her big bag, but she was such a sour-faced woman that Deborah could not believe she would do such a nice thing! She was looking disapprovingly at Grandmother now.

"I thought you was the doctor Mus Puttock. 'e's takin' is time."

Then seeing Deborah's face peering nervously into the room, "I would've thought this was not the place for a child."

"Deborah should see her mother afore she goes to her auntie's," Grandmother Deborah replied firmly, pushing the girl into the room. It did not seem like her parents' room. In spite of the spring sunshine which was beginning to filter in through the blinds, the unfamiliar shadow which the child had sensed in her own room was stronger here. Deborah stood nervously in the middle of the rug, eyeing Mrs. Booker's granite face. Then Mary opened her eyes and looked directly at her daughter. The pall of gloom lifted, Mrs. Booker's grim features receded, and Deborah sprang forward to the bed and clambered onto the eiderdown.

"Oh Deb," whispered her mother. "Be good for your father and Granny won't you? And help with the boys."

"I am good. I will help. Will I be staying at the farm for long?"

"Just for a little time darling," her mother replied. Then her face suddenly creased up again, and Deborah shrank away in fear. But Mary's face softened and relaxed once more. She drew Deborah close to her and whispered so no one else could hear,

"What ever happens, remember how much I love you Deborah."

She winced again, and as Deborah felt herself being lifted from the bed by her father, Mary cried out in pain.

"I'll be back as soon as I can Mary," he called out as he carried his daughter from the bedroom and down the stairs, while she cried into his collar and dripped tears onto his neck.

Outside the inn the cart was waiting, with Beauty standing patiently between the shafts. The sun was newly risen now and the birds sang a chorus to greet the May morning. The green was sparkling with dew and the sweet smell of may blossom hung in the air. Charles placed Deborah on the seat and climbed up beside her. Then Grandmother lifted Tommy up, and he was placed between his father and sister. Finally, the carpet-bag was tucked behind them.

"Up there," Charles called to the horse, and the cart moved away. Deborah glanced across at her home, shining in the late spring sunshine. She looked at her mother's window, and remembered the unfamiliar shadow in the room and her mother's scream of pain. She felt sick and began to cry again. She wanted her father to make a comforting remark, but he just held onto the reins and gazed ahead, his face grim and taut with tiredness and anxiety. Tommy began to cry in sympathy with Deborah, and she remembered she must look after him for Mother, so she put an arm around him as the cart jolted down Westlands Lane towards Soil Farm.

Mary Miles came out as soon as they drew up in front of the house.

"Charles! Is it Mary? How is she?"

Charles passed Tommy down into his aunt's outstretched arms, slowly shaking his head.

"Not good," he said curtly, as he lifted Deborah out of the cart.

"Oh my dear! Have a cup a tea afore you go back."

"No thank 'ee Aunt Mary. I can't 'ang about. I need to be nearby, and there's John Stepney's mare needs shoeing, though Dick can do that if needs be. Don't know if we'll open up tonight. Folks might 'ave to go elsewhere for their ale."

Charles turned the cart and drove out of the yard back up Westlands Lane towards Adversane.

"You had your breakfasts my liddle maids? No! Well you set down and I'll butter some bread for you. I got some nice strawberry preserve you can have for a special treat!"

Inside the kitchen Aunt Jane was eating toast and drinking milky tea.

"We've got visitors Mother," Mary shouted, "Deborah and Tommy has come to see us."

Deborah went over dutifully for the obligatory kiss and the old lady beamed a toothless smile and nodded kindly at the children.

"My, my. You had an early ride today," she quavered.

She was stone deaf and Deborah hated having to shout at her. Whenever they visited Soil Farm Mother told her to speak up nice and loud to Aunt Jane, but when Deborah tried the words came out too quietly for the old woman to hear and she was requested to, "Speak up maid"!

"You can shout when you're at home," Mother reminded her, but it seemed wrong to shout at an adult, for normally that would be considered bad manners.

The day began to look rosier as the sun rose higher. The children played "house" in a corner of the garden. Tommy followed Deborah round, helping her to collect "food" for their larder. Bees from Uncle Hezekiah's hives droned inbetween the wallflowers. Aunt Mary sang hymns as she hung her curtains on the line. It was a day meant for spring-cleaning she said. Ewes and lambs bleated to one another in the adjoining pastures and there was a distant mooing of cows. Aunt Mary's chickens crooned and clucked as they pecked in the farmyard. Uncle Hezekiah came in for lunch, smelling of hay and cattle. He grinned and grunted at the children before tucking into his boiled potatoes and mutton. After lunch Tommy dropped off to sleep on the cushioned settle, keeping company with Aunt Jane, who was dozing in her chair. Deborah sat in the porch with Aunt Mary, who showed her how to knit in garter stitch. She kept dropping her stitches and handing her efforts back to Aunt Mary to be put right. While her aunt explained how to pick up stitches, Deborah gazed at an especially huge bumblebee droning round the fading wallflowers, and wondered what was happening at home and if her mother was feeling better yet.

At bedtime Deborah felt homesick and gazed out of the bedroom window towards Adversane. She thought she could see her father's cart approaching, but it was only Mr. Hard from Nobs Crook. Tommy whimpered for his mother, so Deborah lay down next to him, and they cuddled one another until they both fell asleep.

Next morning was dull and cloudy at first. Deborah helped Aunt Jane to do the breakfast dishes, while Tommy rolled a ball across the flagstone floor, giggling as Ginger – Aunt Mary's tomcat – sprang out at it from different hiding places! Then they heard the gate click and Aunt Mary exclaimed, "It's your Grandma!" as she hurried to open the door.

Grandmother Deborah was looking very tired. She wore a black dress, jacket and hat, and Deborah noticed black ribbons on her sleeves. She began to tremble as she looked at her grandmother's red eyes and nose.

"Set down my dear," said Aunt Mary, placing her sister-in-law in Uncle Hezekiah's big chair.

Tommy ran over to sit on his grandmother's lap, and she beckoned to Deborah to come over too. She came slowly over to the chair and buried her face in the black satin.

"You got to be very brave now Deborah," Grandmother said. "You know your mother was very ill yesterday don't you?"

Deborah nodded into the satin.

"Last night Jesus took her up to heaven to be with him away from her sickness and pain. So we must be happy for her, as she would want us to be."

Deborah's heart felt as black as the satin. She understood what Grandmother had said, but it was hard to believe relating to her own mother. Lucky, their dog, had gone to heaven to be with Jesus and the angels. But he had been a very old dog. Mother had not been an old lady. Old ladies had white or grey hair like Aunt Jane and Grandmother. Terror took hold of her. Whenever there was trouble, Grandmother was always there to help them.

"Oh Granny, you won't go to heaven will you?"

"No, not me yet! I've too much to do. Now look at me Deborah!"

Deborah had left a wet mark on Grandmother's chest where she'd been crying, but Grandmother did not seem to notice. She lifted Deborah onto her lap next to Tommy, who was crying because he knew something bad had happened, and it had spoiled the game he was having with Ginger.

"Jest look after Tommy and be a liddle mother to him now, and the others. We all need to look after one another – that's what your mother wanted."

It was decided that the children should stay where they were until after the funeral, and Grandmother had a lot to do at home, so after a strong cup of tea she left Deborah and Tommy with Aunt Mary and set off walking back up the lane. Deborah stood and watched the short but indefatigable figure as it grew smaller and smaller until all she could see was a little black dot, which finally disappeared around a bend in the lane.

It was a very strange day. Deborah had to wear a grey dress, which was too hot and tickly once the sun broke through. Aunt Jane and Aunt Mary were very kind to her and Tommy, but Jane kept weeping and exclaiming about the "pore liddle babies with no mother to love them". Aunt Mary left her chores to walk with the children over to the sheep field to see the lambs racing. Deborah walked silently and watched the lambs' joyous antics with a blank expression on her face, trying to grasp the enormity of the situation. Uncle Hezekiah had been told the news. He went about his work even more quiet and withdrawn than usual.

Betty, who came in to help with work in the dairy, was asked to take the children for a walk in the afternoon, after Tommy's nap. They went into Lee Place woods. Betty told them it was called Lee Place because people with leprosy used to live there – "leprosy – like in the Bible!" It was unseasonably hot, and the woods seemed airless. They saw wild strawberries, but not yet ripe. Betty pointed out some orchids. It was sticky underfoot, and Deborah got bitten by a mosquito. The bite itched and itched. On the way back they disturbed an adder, basking on the warm path. It slithered rapidly away into the bushes, but after that they kept their eyes fixed on the path until they reached the main track back to the farm.

When they reached the bridge across the brook they played racing sticks. While they were dropping their twigs in for the final time, Mrs. Hard came up the lane on her way to visit Great-aunt Mary. She walked with them, speaking gently to the children, for she had heard the news. Deborah and Tommy felt safer with her than the youthful Betty. Tommy told her they'd "seed a snake!"

"You be careful in the woods days like this my dears," she warned. "'Tis a terrible spot for snakes is Lee Place."

While Great-aunt Mary and Betty prepared the tea, Mrs. Hard made the children strings of paper dolls by folding up Uncle Hezekiah's old newspaper into a concertina shape, and carefully cutting with Great-aunt's second-best scissors. While the women drank their tea, Deborah made the dolls dance to and fro on the rug, but all the while listened to the adult conversation.

"So the babe's not gone with 'er then?"

"Not yet but 'tis a poor liddle mite I do believe. Charles'll have to find a wet nurse for it."

"Is it a boy or a gal?"

"A boy!"

Deborah leapt to her feet.

"Did Mrs. Booker bring another baby Auntie?"

"Oh child! Talk about liddle pitchers havin' big ears! Children should be seen and not heard, I expect you heard that said afore. Now go and play in the garden with Tommy till I call you in."

Four more days passed. The following evening their father came to see them.

They ran up to him and climbed onto his knees.

"I'll fetch the liddle ones 'ome tomorrow Aunt," he said. "The boys are comin' 'ome too. Be nice to get the fam'ly together again. Thank 'ee for lookin' after 'em."

"You got to get life back to normal fer the children, Charles."

"Well, we can try Mary."

Deborah hugged him and he gave a sudden sob, which was as frightening to the child as it was unexpected. Her father, the blacksmith and landlord of the Blacksmith's Arms, did not cry! She looked up at him anxiously, but he smiled at her in his old manner and she felt reassured.

"You got another liddle brother Deb. He's called Henry and he looks just like our Tommy!"

So next day the children rode back in the cart, waving to Aunt Mary and Aunt Jane for as long as they could see them at the gate!

"The house seems dead," complained Aunt Mary, wiping her eyes on a corner of her apron.

Her mother reached out and patted her on the arm.

"They had to go home Mary!"

"I know, but it'll be so hard for 'em, poor liddle babies."

****

Home was not like home any more. There was a strange young woman in the house with her own tiny baby. She nursed it and Henry for several weeks, but she had a husband and other children in Billingshurst. After a time they could spare her no longer and she went back to her own home and family. Once she had gone life at the inn seemed more like it used to be. Lizzie mostly looked after Henry and the other children, but she got cross when the baby cried and often burst into tears herself.

"'Tis too much for that young gel, Charles," Grandmother said. "You must hire another gel to help with the children."

So Maria Stepney joined them. She was kind and caring, but she was not their mother. Deborah realized she was really not going to see her again. Somehow she had half-expected Jesus to send her mother back after a time. She looked out of the bedroom windows, straining her neck as far as it would go to look up the road in both directions. But Mother had gone.

To make life easier for Lizzie, Grandmother Deborah arranged for John to start attending Miss Baker's school with Deborah. So one summer morning John was reluctantly led by his sister across the road to begin his education!

Miss Baker was very well-intentioned, being a deeply religious lady. She provided a good basic education for the times, for those eager to learn, for the reasonable rate of three pennies per child per week. Deborah had been attending school for over a year and was quickly mastering the basic rudiments of the three r's. John, however, already considered himself his father's apprentice. From the outset he resented having to sit still in Miss Baker's neat parlour, repeating the alphabet or counting beads on the abacus. His first attempts at forming letters on his slate were incomprehensible and although he was not yet five years old Miss Baker made him practice his pot hooks and straight lines with her customary grim determination. The formality of school frustrated him. He longed to exchange the atmosphere of starch, chalk and ink for the friendly, familiar smells of coal, horses and hot metal. He was soon regularly reprimanded for arriving at school with grimy hands, having spent some time in the forge "helping" Charles before being dragged away by an irate Lizzie or frantic Deborah, (who had no desire to be late for school herself, knowing that Miss Baker was quite prepared to wield her cane against the hands or legs of any pupil arriving after the bell had been rung).

Because it was summer, numbers at school were smaller than usual. The register was down from the usual sixteen pupils to just nine, including Deborah and John. Children of small farmers round about often missed school, their help being needed at home. Some parents did not send their children at all. If your son could earn a few pennies scaring birds away from the newly sown fields, or your daughter mind the baby while mother was busy gleaning for extra grain, it was considered more useful than spending money which could not easily be spared in order to learn how to read and write. What use was that to a labourer or a housemaid?

The Puttock's cousin James was ten years old and too useful to be spared at hay-making, so he was not at school during John's first two weeks at Miss Baker's; but his brothers George and William were there, which was some comfort for John! Deborah kept a motherly eye on her small brother, but her friends Alice and Betsy Greenfield were glad to have her company at school again, and she was busy with them during the break time, playing house or skipping with a long rope.

Away from school Deborah's grieving did not diminish. Grandmother Deborah understood better than anyone else what was going on in her grand-daughter's mind. John, George and Thomas, being only four, three and two years old when Mary died, were more easily comforted and distracted. But Deborah, who was almost seven, mourned for her mother till she looked "pekid". Mrs. Puttock kept the child busy, when she was not at school, with a multitude of tasks. After breakfast each weekday that summer Charles went over to the forge with Dick Harding, the apprentice. Deborah went with them, and walked the short distance beyond the forge to her grandmother's house. This was her favourite time of day. She picked up the wicker egg basket and grandmother took a bucket of pig-swill. Together they walked up the garden to the sty, where the two pigs were always squealing for their breakfast! They gobbled it up with such gusto it always brought a smile to Deborah's pale face. She liked to hang over the wall of the sty, scratching the pigs' prickly backs while the animals grunted happily, their snouts in the trough.

Grandmother and granddaughter moved on into the field, where the hens were clucking frantically, awaiting their release into the meadow. Deborah opened the hatches and watched the hens racing out, jostling and pushing and clucking. It was a daily delight to search for the warm, smooth eggs, and to count them as they were carefully laid in the basket. Her grandmother scooped grain out of the barrels next to the coops and handed it to Deborah for her to scatter around. Then she took another scoop and they walked down the short lane to the pond where the ducks were clamouring no less urgently than the chicken had been. Once out of the duck-house they ran, with a rocking movement, down to the water. They were usually too busy up-ending to take much notice of breakfast but the geese, (who took their chance and slept in the rushes), waddled towards Grandmother, hissing and sticking their long necks out until they had had a scattering of grain.

Not all jobs were as much fun, but Deborah dutifully helped Annie with the dishes, cleaned Grandmother's brass, weeded paths and was generally useful. Sometimes she helped in the shop, dusting shelves or finding things for customers. John chose to be with his father and Dick in the forge. If there were horses to shoe, Deborah often joined him. Deborah knew it did not hurt the animals to have the new shoes hammered on, but she still pitied the more nervous beasts, which would rear up at the mere sight of the forge. Her father knew his customers well, and if the horse was likely to be overly frisky he would warn the children off. Then they watched from a distance as the horse's owner attempted to calm the frantic beast. Quite often it was only their father's firm and confident handling which could pacify it.

Deborah often played with Alice and Betsy, who lived at Griggs. Sometimes cousin James walked up from Hadfold to escort her and John back to the farm, where they played riotous games in the hay-barn and in the woods.

But she sometimes chose to play alone, seeking out a quiet

corner in her own or Grandmother's garden, where she would make a house for her wooden doll, which she had renamed Mary after her Mother. The doll had been a gift from her parents the Christmas before Mary died.

At bedtime Deborah's heart ached with her loss, although she sometimes realised, with a mixture of fear and panic, that she could not always summon the image of her mother's face into her mind. It was easier to remember how it had felt to be close to her, sitting on her lap, listening to the stories which sometimes continued for weeks on end – a new instalment each night! The children were often the heroine and heroes of these adventures – encountering giants, dragons and fairy princesses who lived in sumptuous castles! Mother sang to them, too, and Deborah remembered the songs and sang them to her brothers. She tried to make up stories, and although she was sure they were not half as good as Mother's had been, Father seemed to enjoy them and said they were good enough to be in The Sunday Book.

Summer passed into autumn. School began again and numbers increased slightly as a handful of children made their way over the fields from distant farms to Adversane, often arriving with hands too chapped to comfortably hold a chalk stick or a pen, and toes sore with chilblains from wearing soaking wet, leaky boots. As winter over-took autumn their attendance dropped off again. Christmas was approaching and Miss Baker read the story of Jesus' birth to the children. They learned Christmas carols, Miss Baker accompanying them on her piano! Deborah's eyes often strayed towards that piano – a masterpiece of fretwork and candelabra – which no-one was allowed to touch except Miss Baker herself. On the last day of term each child received a small cake and a halfpenny to take home, by way of celebration.

At the Blacksmith's Arms Charles was feeling deep concern over his youngest child, for baby Henry was a sickly infant and with the coming of winter he had grown sicklier - permanently choking and wheezing and with a pitifully small appetite. The doctor shook his head over the baby who was gasping for breath as Grandmother Deborah held him over her shoulder close to a cloud of steam

issuing from a large pan on the range.
"You're doing all you can, Mrs. Puttock. If you can nurse him through the winter he'll gather strength I feel sure."

Attempting to coax some groats into her grandson's resisting mouth, Deborah Puttock wished she might share the doctor's optimism.

It looked set to be a quiet and sad Christmas, with Mary's presence missing from the celebrations. Grandmother's sister Maria and her husband, George Puttock, (a prosperous timber merchant), invited the family to spend the day with them in Billingshurst. Baby Henry was rather better, so he was left at home with Maria Stepney, Lizzie and Annie. Dick Harding had been granted a holiday to visit his family at West Chiltington.

The family travelled in the large cart from Adversane to Billingshurst, where there was a gathering of the Puttock's relatives. The Miles and Greenfields did not come, having to look after their livestock. But Uncle James was there with Aunt Rhoda and their daughters, and Uncle John – a grocer in Billingshurst village - came with Aunt Ann. Uncle George and Aunt Maria's son, Thomas, was there, with his wife, Lizzie, and Uncle Edwin and Aunt Maria with their children. Aunt Lizzie made a great fuss of Charles' children, admiring Deborah's new matching hat and muff, (her present from Grandmother), exclaiming over the sturdiness of the older boys and sweeping Tommy into her arms! The Puttocks' house had been decorated throughout, with bright bows of red ribbon and branches of greenery above the pictures and over the doorways. Jugs and vases of berried holly cheered the darkest corners. A huge bunch of mistletoe hung from the door into the dining-room, where a long table was laid for dinner. The sideboard was covered in bowls of apples, filbert nuts and a pyramid of oranges. Logs blazed in the fireplace, and by mid-afternoon candles flickered on mantelshelf and window ledges.

All the company gathered round the long table for a substantial Christmas dinner, with roast beef and vegetables and plum pudding, (which Tommy did not like). After the meal everyone crowded into the drawing room, where a Christmas tree stood grandly in one corner, its sweetly-scented boughs decorated with sweets, ornaments and the small bright flames of tiny candles. Presents for the children had been placed beneath it. Deborah was given a toy teaset, John and George each received a box of metal soldiers and Tommy had a little cart to tow along. Well pleased with their presents, the older children settled down to play dominoes and Happy Families, while John, George and Tommy played with their new toys, taking turns at loading the soldiers into the cart and pulling it round the room. Meanwhile the older generation had gathered round the fireplace. There the story-telling began, followed by singing – songs which had been handed down from one generation to the next. Eventually the children were drawn into the circle, and Deborah was persuaded to sing the carols she had learned at school. She looked down at the floor to steady her nerves, aware of the adult eyes turned towards her, (some of which silently wept a tear as they remembered the one who was missing from their circle).

"She's so like her poor mother," whispered Maria to Grandmother Deborah, who pressed her lips together and quietly nodded her agreement.

When the time came to leave the children were well wrapped in warm blankets and tucked down into the cart. It was very late. The stars were brilliant in the sky – thousands of them shone out in the cold, frosty night. Deborah felt real contentment as she leaned back and gazed up into the never-ending pattern of sparkling lights. She felt full and warm and safe. For the first time since her mother's death she felt really happy and at peace. The scream of a vixen hunting across the fields at Andrews Hill failed to make her jump, the creak of the trees as they rubbed together in a sudden blast of icy wind did not lead her to suspect ghosts or spooks of any kind were following them. It had been a happy day and she felt life was safe once more.

Deborah's peace of mind was short-lived. As the winter wore on the damp, chill weather and persistent colds and croup from which he was never free, weakened Henry a little more each day. He was a pale, thin scrap of a child – each day a little paler, a little thinner. Grandmother Deborah watched over him night and day, neglecting her other duties, but on the morning of 15th February, 1857, Henry stopped breathing.

24

Chapter Two

Apart from the vicissitudes of life which touch every family at some time or another, news within Adversane was rarely any more exciting than a tree blowing down in a gale and blocking the road to Billingshurst. In March 1857, however, Adversane was stirred by a crime which would send tremors from the inconspicuous Sussex hamlet as far distant as the London law courts! Not since the announcement that the London Brighton and South Coast Railway was extending its track from Horsham to Petworth, which meant the imminent construction of a railway house and signal-box at Adversane, had the community been given such a sense of status in the parish! What was more, Charles Puttock was initially implicated in this criminal episode. As it transpired, the incident had a positive effect on the Puttocks, for it so overwhelmed the entire household it helped them to let go of the pain of losing baby Henry.

Alfred and Dennett Allen owned three farms and five malthouses in all, including the one at Adversane. They were well acquainted with Charles, especially Dennett, who lived at nearby Gay Street. He often sank a pint in the the Blacksmith's Arms, claiming the quality of the beer was due to the excellence of the malt used in the brewing! Charles' beer was supplied by the Maltings brewery in Billingshurst who, like most of the local brewers, bought their malt from the Allens because no other maltsters offered such good quality malt as such a low price. It was said that the brothers were worth thousands of pounds, and on many occasions the Blacksmith's Arms' clientele had spent some time contemplating, over their pints of ale, how the Allens managed to pay more than any other maltsters for their barley, yet sold the malt so cheaply! Charles surmised they were up to some trickery, but Dennett was a cheerful and generous-spirited man, and Charles kept his thoughts to himself when his customers got onto the subject of Dennett and Alfred's fortune.

Around two o'clock one morning Charles and his household were woken by the sound of fists banging on the back door of the

Blacksmith's Arms. Charles pushed open the shutters and leaned out of the window with a lantern, blearily trying to penetrate the gloom beneath to see who was there before going down. It was Dennett Allen.

"Charles – can you come down? Quick, man, quick!"

Charles stumbled into his breeches, shirt and jacket and hurried out of his bedroom, sending the rest of the household, who were congregated on the landing, back to their beds.

"It's someone for me. Nothing to worry about," he assured them, running down the stairs, while Dennett hammered harder.

Charles unbolted the door and looked without much enthusiam at his friend.

"What the deuce do you want at this time of night? If there's trouble I want no part of it. I've enough of my own."

"Charles, don't ask me any questions then you won't have to answer any," Dennett swiftly replied. "All I ask is can I borrow some waggons and horses?"

"I got two waggons but only one horse Dennett, t'other one's Mother's."

"Okay, just the waggon then - and the one horse."

"When?"

"What?"

"When d'you want 'em?"

"Now man. That's why I'm standing here. It's urgent. Very urgent."

Charles scratched his head.

"I dunno. I got me fam'ly to think of. I don't want no more trouble than what I've already got."

"I know, Charles. But I'm des'prate for transport. I'll pay you well."

"No Dennett. Take 'em and make sure you don't damage 'em. But I don't want any money. I'd rather keep out of this - whatever it is."

Charles led the men round to the stable and cart shed.

"You got any rope Charlie?" Dennett suddenly asked.

Charles shook his head, but went to a shed and came out

with a large coil of rope which he silently handed to Dennett.

"Thanks Charlie – I won't forget this."

Charles turned his back and went indoors, bolting the door behind him.

Upstairs he found Maria, Lizzie, Dick Harding and all his children gathered in Deborah's room, (which was at the front of the inn), peering out of the shutters at the malthouse.

"What's happening Pa?" asked Deborah, who had been scared at first by the banging on the door, but was now enjoying the novelty of having the entire household congregating in her room to spy on the mysterious activities going on at the malthouse in the dead of night.

Charles swore under his breath.

"I've lent Dennett the horse and big waggon but I don' want any of you to let on I 'ave - an' I don' know what trouble e's got hisself into!"

"We wunt say a word Mr. Puttock, will we?" assured Lizzie, appealing to the others, who were too busy trying to see what was happening outside to answer.

Charles curiosity got the better of him.

"Mind out Maria – let me see!"

By the dim light of the stars, a half moon and the occasional flare of a lantern, (which was quickly covered up again), they could just see figures moving outside the malthouse. A door opened, and a swift ray of light momentarily revealed a line of waggons, which were apparently being loaded with sacks of malt.

"Where are they going?," whispered Maria.

Silently, their wheels muffled by the ropes wound about them, the dimly revealed carts began to leave in a ghostly convoy, crossing the road to Billingshurst and heading towards Newbridge.

"Well, I'll be damned!" exclaimed Charles.

"What are they doing?" Deborah asked.

"They're gettin' rid of their malt, that's what they're doin'." Charles replied.

Then quickly – "But we don't know anything now Deb'rah! You'm not to tell a soul."

****

Dennett might have saved himself the trouble of trying to silence his activities. Next day it transpired everybody knew of the mysterious goings-on at the malthouse. Grandmother Deborah, who had herself been watching the surreptitious removal of the malt, had an early morning visit from her brother, who farmed near the Newbridge Wharf.

"You want malt for your pigs, Deborah, you want to get down to the river. Allens have bin tippin' their malt in there all night, jest about. There's folk comin' from Billings'urst and Wisbro' and all about gettin' it out and takin' it away in barrows and carts!"

Deborah tutted.

"You can jest see me doing that!" Deborah replied with dignity. "We always thought those Allens were up to somethin' tho' didn't we? Always got money to throw about. But they're good employers y'know, so I hear. We'll soon find out a bit more I daresay," (nodding towards the malthouse). "Here come the Revenue!"

Work was abandoned for most of that morning as the community stood respectfully back and watched the drama unfolding in front of them.

The three officers quickly entered the premises, which appeared to be deserted. Within a few minutes one of them reappeared and walked deliberately over to the inn.

"Charles Puttock here?" he demanded.

Deborah went over to him.

"He's in the forge," she said, (Charles having declared he was too busy making some new gates for Caterways to stand about doing nothing!)

The officer disappeared into the forge where Dick and Charles were both working, while little Deborah held tightly to her grandmother's hand and literally shook with fear.

"Don' worry," Deborah reassured the children, all gathered

round her. "Your father is an honest man and he's done nothing to feel guilty about."

Charles looked up with no surprise as the officer entered the forge.

"Can I help you?" he asked, standing up and looking the man straight in the face.

"Charles Puttock?"

"That's me Sir,"

"I believe you are a friend of Messrs. Alfred and Dennett Allen?"

"I know them through my work, Sir. I've shoed Dennett's horses and sold them my ale."

"Where do you purchase your ale Mr. Puttock?"

"From the Maltings in the village, Sir, same as most publicans hereabout."

"Do you know what was 'appening here last night Mr. Puttock?"

Charles replied cautiously, "Well, somethin' was certainly goin' on opposite Sir. Bit of noise. Saw some movement goin' on."

"You got horses and waggons Mr. Puttock?"

"I have one horse and some waggons and a cart Sir."

"I bin told your horse and waggon was out las' night."

"Oh."

"Yes, Mr. Puttock. It was seen leavin' the inn and goin' across to the malthouse!"

Charles stood quietly, waiting.

"What was you doin' out in the night Mr. Puttock?"

"I weren't out, Sir," Charles protested.

"Your horse and waggon didn't move then?"

Charles looked thoughtful for a minute.

"Yessir. I did lend 'em to Mr. Allen."

"What time was that then?"

"I don't know. I jest got to bed and off to sleep and he woke me wanting to borrow the waggon and horse. Wanted them for business purposes I b'lieve."

"What kind of business would that be Mr. Puttock?"

"I really don' know, Sir. I asked no questions. He's a friend of mine. I trust him."

"A friend? More of a business acquaintance you said just now."

"A friend – but not a close friend."

"So you don't know what everyone here seems to know?"

"I bin workin' since six o'clock Sir."

"Do you have any objection to my taking a look round your property Mr. Puttock?"

"None Sir. None whatsomever."

Charles came out of the forge, leaving Dick standing nervously at the anvil, hammer still clutched tightly in his fist.

"I'd like to see your house first," the officer continued,"I must just get one of my officers to join me."

Charles stood silently waiting until the two men returned from the malthouse.

Then he led them inside and there followed a quick but thorough search of the inn, from the attic to the cellar. Here the officers lingered for some time. They shifted the barrels away from the walls and carefully inspected the entire area, while Charles stood watching them with no apparent sign of concern.

After a time they left the house and visited the stable and cart shed. The horse and waggon having been left unceremoniously at the rear of the inn just after 5 o'clock that morning, Charles and Dick, (who had not been back to bed), had quickly got to work. Charles fed and watered Beauty and put her in the meadow while Dick removed the filthy, worn rope from the waggon wheels. Now, with a cursory glance at the stable, the officers moved into the cart shed. The younger officer made for the nearest waggon, climbed up into it and immediately picked something up in his hand.

"No need to ask you what this is I'm sure Mr. Puttock?" he asked, turning to show a palmful of malt.

"No indeed Sir," replied Charles.

"What does this suggest to you then?"

"That malt has been carried in my waggon, Sir, but not by me I have to say!"

"Mr. Puttock, you seem to be a pretty wealthy man for an inn-keeper."

"Not just an inn-keeper, Sir, but a master farrier also. And my family is fortunate in being comfortably off, Sir. We have a lot of property and land hereabouts, though 'tis true I'm not as fortunate as my uncles, Sir. Not in that respec'."

The officers looked at him with genuine suspicion. For the first time Charles began to feel alarm building deep within him, but he was not going to show his concern. He was an innocent man, but he feared there might be some evidence which they felt connected him to the crime.

"We'll let you get back to work then, Mr. Puttock. But we may need to talk to you again."

"That's no problem, Sir. I'll be here."

The officers soon mounted their horses and headed southwards out of Adversane. With them rode the maltster, John Peskett. Charles stood at the edge of the road, watching them until they were dots on the horizon. It was not until they disappeared over the brow of the hill at Brinsbury that he breathed a sigh of relief and without further ado strode over the road to the malthouse. A small crowd was gathering here, where the centre of attention was the maltster's wife, who was literally wringing her hands in her distress.

"What'll become of us?" she wailed. "John's an honest man, I swear it. What will happen to us now?"

"Come along Jane," Deborah's voice broke in above the babble of voices, some attempting to soothe the hysterical woman, others interrogatory, demanding an explanation of the night's activities and its implications for the Allens and their employees.

"Sure we will find out soon enough," Charles said, helping his mother to make a way through the jostling group for Mrs. Peskett, "but we'd better get Jane home first and foremost."

Deborah and Charles half-carried the distraught woman to her cottage and sat her down by the range.

"I'll get back to work now Mother," said Charles, quickly removing himself from the emotionally charged scene, trusting his mother to soothe the situation and find out a few facts while so doing!

"Charles," Deborah called after him, "send Lizzie over with some chamomile would you?"

"Help your nerves dear," she informed Jane, standing the kettle over the range, where it quickly recommenced boiling.

Jane blankly watched her neighbour as Deborah found her way round the tiny kitchen, discovering tea-pot, cups and saucers.

Then Deborah sat down opposite Jane and took one of her hands in her own.

"Oh Mus Puttock, what'll we do? They be putting my John in gaol."

"Now now Jane, don't take on so. Sure they won't put your John in gaol. It's Alfred and Dennett who need to save their skins I'd guess. Sure they just want to ask John a few questions that's all."

At this point Lizzie arrived breathlessly at the door, clutching a jar of dried herbs.

"Thank you Lizzie. You get back to the children now. Right Jane, we'll both have a cup of this, for my nerves are all in a jangle I must say."

The combined effects of the tea and sympathy soothed Jane sufficiently for her to tell Deborah all that had happened that night.

Apparently they had been woken up by Dennett around one o'clock. John had gone to the door, then returned to tell Jane he had some urgent business which couldn't wait for morning and she was not to worry but go back to sleep.

"But I couldn't sleep, Mus Puttock, now could I?"

"Sure you couldn't. What happened next then?"

"John dressed and hurried out, but I got dressed too and followed 'im down to the malthouse, fer I knew it must be somethin' serious-like."

Jane stopped and sipped her tea, wiped her nose and continued.

"There was Dennett and Bert Woods from Chiltington and a whole lot of men all millin' about and Dennett shouted, "Come on, we got to shift the malt as fas' as we can afore the Revenue gets 'ere." They started passin' sacks of malt along and John took 'em out the door and dumped 'em on the green. So I was wondrin' where did they find so much malt and thort I'd go in a bit further. They was all so busy they didn't 'ave time to say nothin' to me and it were dark in there beside. So I went along a bit to the end of the building and there were a gert 'ole in the wall what seemed to go down-like, into a cellar. There were a lantern down there and I could see Dennett workin' 'arder than e's ever worked I'd say, 'eavin' out sack after sack of malt."

Jane paused and stared at her lap.

"Did 'e see you watchin'?"

"No, fer 'e was workin' like a madman. I jus' went back along and I seed John and 'e said, "What you doin' 'ere? You be better off at 'ome." So I said, "Do 'ee be careful John, fer you don' want to be in trouble", an' 'e said, "Tis too late fer that I'd say...."

Jane's voice trailed away and she began crying again, but quietly, then concluded,

"So I wen' 'ome but there was 'orses an' waggons cluttering off down towards Newbridge, all full of malt."

"Well, if you ask me what I think," Deborah said thoughtfully, "Dennett Allen's got himself into deep water, for he must've been hidin' that malt away from the Revenue for some time, and now he and his brother will have a lot of questions to answer. But don't you worry yourself Jane," (leaning forward and patting the wretched woman's hand). "I know 'tis true your John must've known about that malt, but I'll lay he is a very small fish in a big pool an' they won' be too worrid 'bout him. Like I say, the Allens are the ones the Revenue will want to put in gaol. But knowing them, they'll slip out of the net, crafty as they are."

Just as Deborah Puttock stood up to take her leave the Peskett's married daughter came breathlessly through the door, a child hanging onto either hand. The news had carried swiftly round the parish!

Deborah went into the forge to find her son and give him what information she had managed to glean.

"That's why the Revenue men were so interested in the cellar then," Charles said. "They suspect we got a secret store of malt here. Well, they'll be disappointed then, fer they can't pin anythin' on me. I always knew that pair was up to somethin' though, fer it were always a mystery how they made their money."

"I told poor Jane Peskett her John would not have to go to gaol, but I do wonder, for all Allens' men must've known about the hidden malt. I don' think they could really be blamed for keepin' quiet about it, fer the Allens give good wages and who's goin' to turn their back on that?"

"I dunno Mother, but I hopes they'll take pity on the Pesketts, fer they are not as young as they was."

Charles received no more visits from the Revenue, and life went back to normal, although the malthouse stood quiet and empty.

The broadsheets were full of the story, however. Deborah brought her paper into the inn and the entire household gathered round to hear the details. They learned that one of the Allens' employees at the Worthing malthouse had tipped the Excise authorities off, following his dismissal after an attempt to blackmail Alfred and Dennett. Also that £12,000 worth of malt had been seized in all, from the Allens' various malthouses, and taken to the Tower of London.

Charles whistled and leaned back against his chair.

"£12,000 worth!" he repeated, "and then there were all the malt they managed to dump in the river – not that it were there long. Plenty of people were grateful for that malt!"

"Plenty of pigs too," his mother replied with a grin.

"We'll get the full story when the case goes to court," Charles said, laying the paper to one side. "They are going to be tried at the Court of Exchequer in June." He looked thoughtful. "Imagine all that goin' on under our noses."

"Ale's goin' to cost more now," he called over his shoulder as he made his way over to the forge. "Folks won' be too pleased about that!"

****

Spring gave way to summer. The hedges were laden with dog roses and the green golden with buttercups and birds foot trefoil, which the children called apple pie. Farmers cut their grass and clover fields – sending orange tips and meadow browns fluttering away into the safety of neighbouring gardens. Newly sheared sheep looked strangely naked as they grazed the pastures, while their growing lambs still played and bleated.

Charles' children were well and lively under the combined care of his mother, Lizzie and Maria. But one day Maria came to Charles and told him she would be leaving them to get married to Joshua Holmes. He had got a new job as shepherd at Lee Place the previous March and had his own cottage. They wanted to wed as soon as possible so she could look after Joshua and the home they were to have together.

Although the children did not want Maria to leave them, they still had their father, grandmother and Lizzie to look after them. Charles agreed to let Maria go at the end of the month. As he watched Lizzie hastily pegging the week's washing on the line he remembered how hard it had been for her to cope alone before. She was just a girl and with meals to cook, the house and inn to keep clean and four children to mind – especially Thomas who was not yet old enough to go to school – he doubted she would find it easy. He decided to look for another woman to help them. A regular customer recommended his cousin from Storrington – one Mary Hughes. She had never married, but been in service for the same family since she left school more than twenty years earlier. He knew she wanted a change of job. At thirty-four, (the same age as Charles), she was a confirmed spinster. Yes, he would tell Mary's parents there was a job going at the Blacksmith's Arms next time he saw them. They could pass the details on to her. Charles could wait until the message had been given and she had had time to think about it.

Meanwhile the Allens had caused another sensation. Their trial had been set for 16th June, at the Court of Exchequer. The literate amongst the local populace waited for the publication of the details in the broadsheets. What they read was even more exciting than they had anticipated.

As usual it was Grandmother Deborah who first read the news in the Puttock family. She came hurrying round to the inn, clutching her newspaper.

"Just listen to this," she announced, seating herself in the comfiest chair and opening the paper before her. "I always said those Allens would get away with it."

"What now?" called Charles from the bar.

"Do come here Charles – you will never believe what they've done!"

"What's that?" Charles asked somewhat wearily, having had a long morning in the forge.

"They have escaped Charles. They boarded a steamer bound for France, knowing all the while that they was goin' to be followed. The police detectives followed 'em on the next steamer, but they was on their way back to London! Can you believe that? The cheek of those two. While the police looked for 'em in France they had got a boat from Liverpool to the Americas!!"

"Never!" Charles exclaimed, then exploded with laughter. "My Lor' they got some nerve those Allens."

"It says here the case went on without them. They bin fined £110,000, but they won' be paying it will they?"

"Spect they'll make themselves an even bigger fortune in America," Deborah added somewhat resentfully. "Talk about the devil looks after his own!"

By the end of June the malthouse was under new management. John and Jane Peskett moved in with their daughter and her family, all crowded under one roof. But John did not get charged with any offence, perhaps out of respect for his advancing years.

****

Mary Hughes was interested in the vacancy at the Blacksmith's Arms. She travelled to Adversane on the carrier's cart on one of her infrequent afternoons off. She was quiet, stolid and sensible, seemed genuinely fond of children and said she could give excellent references. Charles thought she might be more reliable than a young girl and not likely to go off to wed like young Maria, or perhaps Lizzie in due time. He offered her the job and she accepted. In August she commenced her employment at the inn. The children accepted her: they were used to change in their lives. But young Deborah felt no warmth towards her. She spent as much time as possible with her beloved Grandmother.

At New Year, 1858, Mary had gone to visit her parents. Charles took the opportunity to announce, rather awkwardly, that he had asked her to marry him and she had accepted. The wedding would be in February.

After Charles' marriage to Mary Hughes on 3rd February 1858, life changed little from the previous few months of Mary's employment at the inn, except that she now shared Charles' bed.

No babies were born from this marriage, but Charles' children by his first wife were well cared for and loved by their stepmother. The boys were inclined to be weak-chested and delicate, (although John was determined he would follow his father into the farrier's trade), and Mary made sure they were warmly dressed and well fed. She was a kindly woman, an excellent cook and thorough housewife, and she gave an air of stability to the home which benefited everybody. For Deborah, however, her grandmother remained her substitute mother, and she spent much of her spare time at Sayers – either in the shop or the house.

Although little changed in Adversane, the forward progress of the London Brighton and South Coast Railway continued. There was disappointment from some when it was learned that there would be no station built at Adversane, but relief from others.

"We have the carriers comin' through, so what do we want with noisy trains?" Grandmother Deborah argued with her son. "They be horrible, dangerous objects and we can manage quite well wi'out 'em! And I'm surprised at you, Charles, fer there'll be fewer horses to shoe if folks travel on trains."

Charles looked unmoved.

"Well, Mother, I s'pose that's true to a point. But how will folks get to the stations then? They'll still be wantin' carriages an' carts fer that. Anyways, 'tis progress an' we can't stop it."

"More's the pity," his mother acidly retorted, vehemently pounding the lump of dough she was kneading.

Charles grinned and wandered back over to the forge, where he had left Dick dealing with some of the minor jobs demanded of the farrier. There were always a number of small tasks to be dealt with in between bigger jobs: kettles, pans and tools to mend.

It was a Wednesday morning and Charman's cart was outside the inn. Charman was the Pulborough carrier and travelled through Adversane to Horsham on Wednesdays and Saturdays. The Wisborough Green carrier, Mr. Coombes, passed that way on Mondays, so the hamlet was comparatively lucky when it came to sending and receiving goods from the surrounding area. Charles knew Mr. Charman would be in the kitchen having a cup of tea, as this was a regular occurrence. Most people encouraged the carriers to stop for refreshment along the way, for they not only brought parcels and people to and from the villages, but local news besides!

"'Mornin' Fred, how ye keepin'?" Charles asked, seating himself at the kitchen table opposite the carrier.

"O, fair to middlin', thank 'ee," Fred replied somewhat mournfully, slowly shaking his head to and fro.

"I were jest sayin' Mr. Charman be lookin' pekid today," Mary said, looking keenly at her visitor.

"I be jest puckered-up wi' the cold," he answered, taking a another sip from his steaming mug, "an' I'm so moithered this marnin' I can't git on very fast."

"That don't sound like you Fred," said Charles.

"'Spect I jest be gettin' old," Fred replied sadly.

Fred was always a cheerful man, whose arrival was invariably heralded by the sound of his whistling or singing.

"That's noways like you Fred," said Charles with concern.

"Belikes I will be 'andin' over the carryin' somewhen soon. I can't be upsides with this 'ere railway what's comin'."

"Ah," said Charles, looking relieved. "You don' want to be

worritted 'bout that, Fred. I bin talkin' to Mother 'bout it this very mornin', and I says to you what I says to her, that folks wull still be needin' horses and carriers fer a good many years so fer as I can tell."

"Maybe, but they trains will be to and fro to Horsham a lot faster than my 'orse can trot. Folks'll want to goo wi' them, not the likes of me. They can carry dunnamany people and parcels. They trains'll be comin' through 'ere to Pul'brough an' Petworth in six months yer know."

"Folks don' like the soun' of they trains. They goos too fast fer sensible folks," said Mary. "I shan't be ridin' in 'em fer one!! They be fer town folk not country people."

Fred went on his way somewhat reassured by the loyalty of his customers, which met him at every stop. But in spite of this, excitement grew as the summer gave way to autumn and the opening of the railway became imminent.

The men and boys, especially, spent any spare minutes they could watching the progress of the railway track as it approached Adversane from the north. The gangers worked quickly and the track progressed at speed through Adversane and away into the hazy distance, running parallel to the Roman road and just as straight!

Because the track passed over the road leading east from Adversane towards Broadford Bridge, there had to be a crossing gate. In late summer men began building a cottage for a gatekeeper. The Puttock family's Sunday afternoon stroll often took them past the building site. Standing on the track and gazing towards Billingshurst they could even see the spire of St. Mary's church, very small and blue and far away. By late September all was ready and waiting for the great day when the first train would run through the hamlet. Meanwhile the track and cottage building continued all the way along the route beyond Adversane to Pulborough and far-away Petworth. Although the children had some knowledge of Pulborough, Petworth was as exotic and far-away a place as Timbuctoo! Would they ever be lucky enough to ride in a train as far as Petworth? It was an adventure they longed for!

On October 10th 1859 the railway was opened. The hamlet

took a half-holiday. People came in from outlying farms on foot or by cart or carriage to see their first train, which was actually going to stop at the crossing so the gatekeeper and family could disembark with all their worldly goods. There was a crowd gathered near the new cottage – although most people kept a safe distance between themselves and the track. After what seemed a very long wait to the impatient children, a shout went up from those men and youths brave enough to be standing on the track, looking northwards. For an hour or more they had been imagining a plume of smoke, now it was real!

Even Grandmother Deborah felt excited as the noise of the steam engine was carried towards them along the line.

"Keep away, go right back," men shouted at the children, some of whom had crept nearer the line, but they did not need to be told a second time and beat a hasty retreat as the puffing and roaring of the mighty engine grew closer and louder.

As it drew to a halt the people gazed in amazement at this symbol of a new age. Thus far the industrial revolution had meant little to them. They knew about the changes which were occurring; had heard about the railways and the impact they were having. Those people who could not read got their information from others who could. Now here was the reality in front of their very eyes; a gigantic hissing monster, smelling of coal and steam. The tranquillity of their fields and woods had been invaded by this mighty and powerful machine. It struck fear in the hearts of many of those looking on, for they sensed that they were witnessing the beginning of a deep and lasting change to come for their children and grandchildren.

"Don't you go near it George," Grandmother Deborah exclaimed, grabbing her grandson by the arm as he showed every sign of getting a closer look. "It might blow up!"

Though it was difficult for the on-lookers to take their eyes away from the engine itself, their attention was being drawn to intense activity going on just down the track, where men were unloading the family and chattels of Thomas and Mary Smith, the first residents of the new railway cottage. Besides the gatekeeper's tools of the trade, such as fog lamps and flags, four children, two dogs, a crate of chicken, beds and bedsteads, tables and chairs, bundles of clothes and linen were swiftly and efficiently lifted out of the train, ready to be installed in their home. Thomas was a railway labourer and his wife was to be in charge of the signals and crossing gates. At that moment, she was more concerned with getting her family away from the mighty wheels of the train.

The engine built up steam and moved slowly forward, gradually gathering speed as it snaked away towards Pulborough with its cargo of railway officials and porters, gatekeepers, their families and worldly goods.

The group of people began to disperse slowly, still exclaiming in amazement over the size and noise and speed of the train, while a few remained to help the new residents carry their possessions into the cottage. The Puttock children quickly formed into a train, with John as their engine, and puffed and whistled their way back to the inn, while Grandmother Deborah and Charles and Mary continued to argue about the benefits, or not, of progress.

Chapter Three

Charles's children were bright, but the boys were not very interested in school. Deborah enjoyed her lessons, and Miss Baker frequently passed her work around for the other children to see, while Deborah fidgeted with embarrassment. She had no desire to be singled out and shrank from the unwanted attention!

In the late 1850's Church of England schools were built in nearby North Heath and Nutbourne. In 1861 Miss Baker announced her decision to close her school in Adversane. She had been offered the position of Headmistress at Nutbourne, and was moving to Pulborough. Charles decided his boys should attend North Heath school, which was closer than Nutbourne. Deborah was nearly twelve and nearing the end of her education. In theory she had reached the age where she could be employed as a servant in one of the large houses round about, which fate had already befallen her friend Alice, who was working in the kitchen at Caterways. The Puttocks had different ideas. Deborah knew well the running of her grandmother's shop, and Grandmother Deborah was now 61 and finding she got a lot more tired than she used to do – looking after both the shop and smallholding. Charles and his mother discussed taking Deborah out of school, and preparing her to take over the shop altogether in a few years' time. Charles felt sure his daughter would be delighted by this suggestion, and he called her over to his side one quiet August evening, as he sat on a bench outside the inn taking a few moments away from the bar.

"You know Deb, Grandmother and I have been thinkin' 'bout what's best fer you to do now you are a'most twelve years old and ready to work."

"But I am going to go to North Heath with the boys aren't I?" Deborah immediately replied, alarmed by the possibility of any other idea. "I still have a lot to learn."

"You read and write and do your sums better'n mos' grown-ups Deborah. If you leave school now and start helping Granny in the shop all the time 'stead of just now and then you can larn all about it, and then" – he paused for effect -"it will be your own shop one day!"

Deborah was silent and looked down at her dusty boots.

"Well, what d'you think?"

Deborah traced circles in the dust with the toe of her right boot – round and round and round.

"Well?" Charles asked again, with a hint of irritation in his voice. "Answer then. Cor – I thought you'd be jumpin' up and down with joy!"

"It sounds nice," said Deborah lamely, "but I want to be a school mistress, like Miss Baker, and maybe have my own school, not a shop."

"You ungrateful gel," Charles exclaimed, standing up and towering over her. "You don' know how lucky you are to have the chance."

"I do, I do, but I want to be a teacher. Miss Baker said one day I could be a teacher if I stay at school and train alongside her. But she's going to Nutbourne so I don' suppose I'll ever be a teacher now!"

Deborah bobbed up off the bench and ran as fast as she could in the direction of Sayers. At that moment Grandmother Deborah came out of her gate and started to walk up towards them. The child rushed past her and away towards the meadow, where she had made a special "nest" under a crab apple tree. Here she curled up in a miserable ball and cried so passionately she even surprised herself.

"What's up with our Deb?" asked Grandmother, approaching Charles slowly through the long grasses. "Oh – it's so sultry and airless I thought I'd see if there's any more air out here, but there isn't! What's the matter with her then?"

Charles had sat back down on the bench, his face still red with anger.

"I told her about the shop, Mother, thinkin' she'd be over the moon 'bout it, and she jest sulked a bit, then says, 'oh, but I want to be a school mistress'!"

Grandmother Deborah was quiet for a moment.

"So?" she finally said.

"What d'you mean 'so'?"

"Well, it's no surprise really when you thinks of it Charles. You always encouraged her to make up tales and write and all. You always been proud when Miss Baker said Deborah's her brightest pupil."

"Yes, but workin' in the shop – and knowin' it will be hers to run how she likes ……cor! Thought she would be pleased didn't you then?"

"I hoped she would be, cos it would help me in my old age, and I'd like to think Deb would take it over, but there's others in the fam'ly beside her, and if Miss Baker thinks teaching would be a good job for Deborah I'll say I'd be very proud of our girl."

Charles looked at his mother with respect.

"You'm right as usual," he said. "Think I'll goo over and have a word with Miss Baker tomorrow."

Charles strolled over to Pound House next afternoon and found the teacher seated in the shade, diligently embroidering a table-cloth.

"Mr. Puttock!" she exclaimed, laying her work aside. "Do sit down. Would you like a glass of lemonade? It's very warm again isn't it?"

"No thank ye Miss Baker," Charles replied, perching awkwardly on the edge of a garden seat. "Sorry to intrude on you Ma'am, but I need to talk to you about Deborah."

Miss Baker looked keenly at him.

"She's a bright girl," she said.

"Yes – I knows it and am proud of her. But, you see, I wants her to leave school now and work with my mother in the shop – it will be hers one day. She don' want to. She wants to be a school teacher. What do you think 'bout that idea?"

"I expect she's told you I think she has the potential to be a good teacher. She is a very good all-rounder and practical as well as clever. She's very good with the little ones too. What I would suggest, Mr. Puttock, if you are happy to allow her to continue at school for a few more years, is that she works as a monitor or pupil teacher until she is sixteen. Then she can be a school mistress and perhaps have her own school – as I have had all these years."

Charles felt pride rise up within him and began to warm to this new idea.

"So could she do that at Nutbourne Ma'am?"

"If not there, then North Heath or Pulborough."

"Bit of a long way – Pulborough," Charles said thoughtfully. "She could walk to North Heath or even Nutbourne, but Pulborough's a bit further. Still, Dick or I could take her over in the cart maybe."

"I am going to visit Miss Odell at Nutbourne this week, to discuss the work I shall be doing there. I will mention Deborah to her. If she has insufficient room I will speak to Miss Dallimore at North Heath," Miss Baker replied.

Charles walked briskly back over to the inn, where Deborah was hovering near the door, waiting for him to return.

"I'm thinkin' 'bout it," he said, with a grin. Deborah's heart jumped. She felt hope rising up within her. She followed her father into the inn where her step-mother was making jam. It was very hot and Mary's usually equable temper rather frayed.

"Where you bin Deborah?" she demanded. "I need you to wash out some more jars fer me – we got so many plums. And how did you get on then Charlie?" turning to her husband. Mary knew about Charles visit to Miss Baker. She disapproved of the idea of Deborah becoming a teacher when she was fortunate enough to have a shop of her own in the offing.

"Miss Baker thinks it would be a good thing fer Deborah to go on and be a teacher as she has the brains to do it and I agrees with that. We can afford it," Charles replied, helping himself to some ginger beer from the cool larder.

"Pa," squealed Deborah, turning away from the cupboard and leaping over the jam jars which she had been assembling like soldiers.

"Now I must do some work in the forge – I wasted enough time fer one arternoon."

Charles quickly disappeared. Mary looked crossly at

Deborah.

"Well, where's those jars? Put 'em in the oven to warm and then see if your grandma has any more plums fer jam-making. You'm not a school marm yet yer know."

"Yes Mary," said Deborah. Then she suddenly went up to Mary and hugged her. As Deborah was not given to displays of affection towards her step-mother, Mary was taken aback by this sudden show of warmth.

"You'll make a good teacher, Deborah," she said kindly. "I can just see you doin' it!"

****

In the first week of September all four Puttock children set out early to walk to their new school, Tommy tearfully hanging onto Deborah's hand and regularly looking longingly back towards Adversane as the familiar cluster of houses diminished in size. They reached the top of the hill at Brinsbury and the distant hamlet was lost from view.

"It's only a little bit further Tom," John tried to reassure him. "In a minute you'll see the school, remember."

Secretly John's legs were feeling slightly wobbly at the prospect of starting a new school. His spirits were only kept aloft by the comforting thought that he would be working in his father's forge the following year. Charles had promised John he might leave school after his eleventh birthday so long as he worked hard at his school work now. Dick Harding was coming to the end of his apprenticeship and wanted to move on, and John had proved his skill in the forge in spite of his small stature, so Charles was keen to have his son working alongside him.

The children had been taken by their father to meet Miss Dallimore the previous week and had formed the impression she would not stand for any nonsense. It would certainly not do to arrive late, especially on their first morning, so Deborah and John each took hold of one of Tommy's hands and pulled him till his dragging walk changed into a trot, while George ran ahead urging Tom to catch him up! George's equable temperament was rarely upset and he was enjoying the novelty of the occasion.

As they drew near the school they joined a straggle of children, none of whom they recognised, who stared at the Puttocks and whispered together. Deborah was older than most of them, however, and resented their blatant curiosity. Why should they be stared at just because they were new to the school? She had inherited her grandmother's sense of dignity and stared fixedly and coolly back.

"Wot you starin' at?" then shouted one of the boys.

"Could ask you the same," retorted John boldly.

It was not a good start.

However, they followed their new schoolfellows into the playground and stood together in a protective huddle. Immediately a bell began to ring in the little tower on the roof of the school and the children began walking inside. "This", George whispered to John, "is a real school!" But after Miss Baker's room the classroom they entered seemed vast and the group of some thirty children a bewildering crowd. Deborah felt sick with nerves and wondered if she could she really be a school mistress and look after a huge class like this? But Miss Dallimore was talking to them and telling them to sit down – in any seat for now. She would be sorting them out according to age shortly and then the new children would be asked to do some tests for her.

John looked at George and sighed!

****

For a brief time each September, Adversane became the focal point of the entire parish of Billingshurst and beyond, for its charter fair was the event of the year. The common land all about the crossroads was covered with stalls and booths and outside the Blacksmith's Arms whole sheep were roasted. It provided a rare opportunity for local people to sell and buy as well as enjoy themselves.

As the Puttock children dawdled home from school during the first weeks at North Heath, weary and with their heads full of new impressions, they were over-taken by a line of caravans and waggons. Dark-skinned mothers nursed babies and small children, sitting up behind the horses, while long-legged men and big boys and girls walked and ran alongside.

"It's the fair!" the boys shouted, their pace increasing to keep up, though Deborah drew George and Tommy close to her and looked nervously at the dogs which loped and sniffed around them.

"Hurray – it's the fair!"

The boys broke away and danced about with whoops of joy – it was exactly what they needed to drive out the stifling atmosphere of school! Forget about tomorrow – the fair was coming to Adversane! They were saved!

They hurried down the hill from Brinsbury Farm. In the distance the tiny hamlet was being transformed into a village. As they drew closer they could see caravans and carts drawn up all along the verges. Horses grazed on the green next to the inn and children and dogs ran everywhere. Spirals of smoke arose from fires as the women began boiling their kettles. The grass in front of their home was filling with new arrivals, and the Puttock children made their way between the bustle of carts, animals and strangers with an odd sense of being in another place altogether. It was thrilling and they all ran indoors high as kites with excitement.

"Hello, hello," Mary greeted them warmly. "How did you get on today?"

But not even Deborah wanted to talk about school.

"Can we go out and look at the fair?" the boys pleaded the moment they were in the door.

"There's nothing to see yet," Mary said. "They wun't be putting up their dobbies till tomorrow!"

"We want to see what's goin' on," John insisted, wondering – not for the first time – why grown-ups were sometimes so dull?

"I don' know," said Mary doubtfully. "You better ask your father. I don' trust they cart people. They be a lot of thieves an'," (with lowered voice), " they sometimes steals childern."

Charles made no objection to the boys looking around, so long as the three of them stayed together and were back in an hour for their tea. Deborah wanted to see her Grandmother and would be needed to help Mary get the meal ready before long. She stole five minutes to watch the scene unfolding from her bedroom window. Her brothers were standing in a small huddle watching some men who were already putting up a booth on the grass to the north of the inn. A woman and girl were slicing vegetables into a cooking pot, while a small child crawled around on the grass next to them, chewing a slice of raw potato.

What would it be like to travel from place to place in a covered waggon or a proper caravan, making your home wherever you stopped – in a wood, by a river, on a village green or common? Deborah imagined herself living such a life. She would make clothes pegs and windmills and tell fortunes. Each year she would come here to Adversane and then go off again – to places she had read about in school. She would travel all the way up to Scotland – to see mountains and lakes and forests and men wearing kilts!

"Deborah – you there? You should be helpin' Grandma!" her father shouted up the stairs.

Deborah ran downstairs and across the grass to the shop. She always looked in on Grandmother and helped her with any chores that needed doing before going back to give Mary a hand.

This afternoon Grandmother was anxious to get her poultry shut in promptly for the night.

"There's more than foxes to worry about fer the next few nights," she said knowingly.

The local people welcomed the fair, but they knew it was prudent to put under lock and key anything that might have a use for the gypsies. Not all of them were untrustworthy, but most of the cart people were opportunists at the very least. Charles carefully secured his forge at night, as far as possible fruit and vegetables were harvested and shut away before fair week and it was not a good idea to leave ducks and hens out unwatched. The men from the fair were notorious poachers, but the local gamekeepers were afraid of them and the cudgels they invariably carried. The scent of roasting pheasant and rabbit stew often wafted over from the gypsy camps, but people knew better than to ask where the meat had come from! It was a known fact that the local game population would be significantly reduced during early September!

With great reluctance the children walked to school next day, only comforted by the knowledge that the fair would be up and running by their return in the late afternoon. While they recited poetry, practiced their handwriting and added up bills the fair was taking shape at home – sideshows, boxing, dancing and drinking booths, Aunt Sallies, swing-boats and hand-driven dobby horses were being assembled, until the grass was barely visible between them. In addition to the fun side of the fair, there was the business side – which was more important to most people. There were stalls selling all manner of wares – generally much cheaper than could be had from local tradesmen though not necessarily of such good quality! By the afternoon people had come into Adversane to buy. In general animals were no longer traded at the fair as they had once been, because farmers bought and sold stock at Pulborough market or Findon Fair, but there was some business done buying and selling pigs and poultry. Animal products were for sale in plenty – wool, (spun and unspun), cheese from cows and goats, butter and eggs, brawn and bacon. Men bought tools and livestock feed. Women had been carefully saving money back for weeks for bales of cloth and cottons to make clothes for themselves and their families. There were stalls selling cheap toys, which might be put away secretly until Christmas – wooden dolls and soldiers, monkeys on sticks, windmills. For a treat there were gingerbread stalls, and sweet stalls selling toffee, black jack, comfits, sugar sticks – there was plenty to tempt children and adults alike.

The children had to wait until Saturday before they could enjoy the fair properly, however. Until then they could only watch the proceedings from the bedroom windows, as it was not permitted for them to roam round on their own. The entire adult household was run off its feet coping with the extra business the fair brought to the Blacksmith's Arms and had no time to take the children to the sideshows. Besides, the rule had always been that no pennies would be handed over until Saturday, for Saturday was the glorious climax of the fair's short season. More entertainers arrived in Adversane during that day, and local people converged on the hamlet in droves from every direction. Bill Grinsted, Maurice Greenfield, Uncle Hezekiah and his son John came to help at the Blacksmiths' Arms, where whole sheep were roasted on spits just outside the inn. With the ale flowing inside and locals rubbing shoulders with a large company of strangers, the atmosphere became highly charged. Deborah, John, George and Tom could barely contain their excitement as the clamour and noise filled every corner of the inn and merged with the hubbub outside.

Deborah ran across to Sayers after tea, to see if she could persuade her grandmother to go to the fair.

"Uncle Hezekiah and Aunt Mary are coming," she said, hopping from one foot to the other.

"Maybe, but I'd rather stay put and get on with makin' my feather bolsters. Now you go and enjoy yourself, for I'm about to bolt the door."

"But there's even a wild beast show this year, Grandmother."

"That sort a thing don't appeal to me these days, Deborah. I'll be glad when it's Monday and they'll be on their way," snapped Grandmother, moving meaningfully towards the kitchen door and putting a hand on the heavy bolt. She had shut her shop early in case there was trouble. The poultry were already cooped up and she wanted to settle down for a long evening.

"But it'll be so boring when they've gone," Deborah complained. "We'll have to wait another year for it to come back."

"Good thing too," Grandmother crossly retorted. "When you are a grown woman you'll understand more all the trouble it brings with it. Men drinking too much, brawling and bad language. It's when you're tucked up in bed the real trouble starts. Now you get along and let me lock this door."

Deborah knew argument was in vain when Grandmother was in that mood, so she hurried back through the swelling crowds into her own kitchen, which was full of people. Mary Puttock was drinking tea with Great-Aunt Maria, Aunt Maria Grinsted from Hadfold, Aunt Mary from Soil (who was nursing Maria's baby son, Alfred), and her daughter Mary, a young lady of nineteen. She worked in the household of Stephen Evershed, a local vet, but had an evening off to visit the fair. Mary was looking very pretty, dressed in her best dress, hat and jacket and flushed with the heat from the fire and the rapid beating of her heart. It raced uncontrollably every time she thought about Frederick Carter, who was walking up from Nobs Crook, where he was shepherd! William, Charles and Emily Grinsted fidgeted and shuffled their feet impatiently, all squeezed together on the settle, facing John, George and Tommy on the opposite side of the fireplace.

"It's Debra," shouted Emily, jumping up. "Now can we go to the fair?"

"We are waitin' fer Uncle George," replied her mother calmly.

Luckily there followed a knock on the inner door and Uncle George appeared from the region of the bar, beaming from ear to ear. His excitement was not much less than that of the children.

"Everybody ready then?" he asked, rapping the floor with his cane.

The children were ready instantly, but had to wait while Maria wrapped Alfred in a shawl the better to carry him round the fair, it being his bedtime and his head nodding in the warmth from the cooking range.

At last everyone was organized and the party left the protective walls of the inn and headed into the babbling, raucous crowd. The sun was dipping down, but it was early September and a clear evening, so still a lot of light in the sky. In between the booths and stalls, however, it was growing dusky and the naphtha lights were already being lit.

Hezekiah's daughter, Mary, followed the others slowly, looking from right to left for a glimpse of Fred. He had said he would meet her near the inn, but there was such a press of people round the roasting spits and, anyway, he might not have arrived yet.

"Can we go to the menagerie Uncle George? I want to see the wild beasts – there might be a real lion yer know, 'cos Jim Knight says so!" John shouted, running backwards in front of his uncle and colliding with a gossiping farmer, spilling some beer from the man's tankard.

"Watch it young man," the farmer yelled, none too pleased.

"Oh the dobbies, please the dobbies," the girls pleaded.

"We'll see it all in good time," Mary Puttock said, firmly holding onto Tommy's hand. "Let's jest make our way round."

" I'll catch up with you later Mother," young Mary Miles suddenly exclaimed, seeing Fred waving at her from a few yards away.

Mary looked at her daughter's face, which had flushed a deeper shade of pink, and smiled as she saw Fred pushing his way through the crowd towards them, returning his greeting.

"You have a good time, Mary, and we will see you back in the Arms if you don' find us roun' the fair."

"Ow, where's Mary goin'?" complained Emily, looking back at her grown-up cousin.

"She's got a young man. Don' stare so Em'ly," Deborah replied. "Look – I can see the dobby horses over there!"

Mary looked shyly up at Fred, who was wearing his best waistcoat and jacket, his face still glowing from his walk into the hamlet and the pints of ale he had already downed.

"You look very nice Fred," Mary said, admiring his new waistcoat.

"You look very pretty Mary," he replied rather awkwardly. "Well, what s'all we do first then? Do'you want a ride on the swing-boats?"

"Let's have a look at the stalls Fred. I might buy myself somethin' new to wear."

"Whatever you like," Fred answered, trying to hide his disappointment.

"'It won't take long and then we can go to the sideshows," she smiled, slipping her hand through his arm.

Together the couple wandered round the fair, Fred full of

pride at the admiring glances Mary received from the friends and relations they met, Mary equally proud of her tall and handsome escort. Fred stood by as Mary browsed along the stalls of knick-knacks and cheap jewellery, but she bought nothing more exciting than a pair of gloves. Then they paused to eat some gingerbread and drink some lemonade (Mary) and ale (Fred), before continuing to move round the attractions. By now it was dark and even more crowded than it had been. The atmosphere became increasingly vibrant and unreal. They were not accustomed to the press of people, the shouting of the booth-owners and showmen. They were caught up on the tide of excitement and moved almost recklessly from one thing to another, exclaiming in amazement at the wild animals in the menagerie and the fearlessness of the fakir, who lay down on a bed of nails and walked over hot coals. At one edge of the fair they came to a dancing booth, where a German band was playing.

"Let us dance Fred," Mary exclaimed, grabbing his arm and pulling him forwards.

"I ain't much good at dancin' Mary," he pleaded.

In spite of her pestering he would not be persuaded.

"I can't dance Mary," he insisted.

No amount of cajoling would make him change his mind. Mary watched some of her acquaintances polkaing with their sweethearts and she felt suddenly resentful and hard done by. Fred had not even bought her a present at the stalls – only some gingerbread and lemonade.

Fred looked uneasy.

"What else would you like to do Mary?"

"I don' know. I feels rather tired."

"Well, you won' want to dance then. How about another drink? I could use a pint of ale!"

"No thank you Fred," she answered rather stiffly. Then she felt ashamed of herself, as he looked uncomfortably down at her. "Perhaps I will then," she replied.

They had another drink and began to make their way back along the edge of the fair towards the inn.

"Swing-boats Mary," Fred pointed out.

"All right. But not too high," she consented.

He helped her in, with rather a lot of giggling and some difficulty arranging her skirts.

To and fro they swung. Mary felt she was being very daring and wondered whether she should be doing this. Her mother would probably think she was being fast and not very lady-like. One hand, wearing a new glove, rested on her knees, ensuring her skirts covered her legs.

The ride stopped and they moved off, Fred with his arm around Mary's waist. Increasingly relaxed and abandoning herself to the magic of the evening, Mary leaned against him as they walked on.

They came to the boxing booth, where a hoarse voice was inviting people to see the champion boxer fight anyone brave enough to face him.

"Cor, I want to see this," Fred said, hurrying towards it.

"Oh no Fred, I hate such things," Mary exclaimed. "I hate fighting. It's horrible."

"No – it's a skill Mary!"

"But I hate it. I hate to see blood. Please don't Fred."

"Mary, I went with you to all the stalls while you looked at the clothes an' all."

"That was different. And you wouldn't come dancin' with me in the dancin' booth."

"Well, I can't dance can I?"

"And I can't stand seeing men hurt one another, like wild animals."

They faced one another – Fred determined and Mary affronted.

"The fight's about to start," the showman yelled. "Anyone else to see the amazin' agility and strength of The Champ and the amazin' courage of his opponent? Can anyone beat the boxing champion? We say 'e's unbeatable. We invite you to prove us wrong, gen'lemen. Knock 'im out fer a count of ten or make 'im give in – either way you can win a guinea gen'lemen. Come and see the brave man who's volunteered to give it 'is all."

One of Fred's friends suddenly appeared at their side.
"'ullo Fred. D'you know that's Bob Farhall in there?"
"'ullo Bert. Cor – Bob Farhall? Goin' to fight The Champ? No! This I must see. C'mon Mary."
For a moment she hesitated, then allowed herself to be pulled towards the hollering showman. He quickly took Fred's money and continued his shouting as they stumbled through the tarpaulin door into the booth. A biggish crowd, all men, stood round the roped-off ring. It was full of trampled straw. There was a smell of sweat and beer. Fred stopped and looked down at Mary – suddenly aware of the situation they were in. She stared resentfully up at him, eyes full of reproach.
"Only this one match, Mary. I jest want to cheer on ol' Bob."
The shouting stopped and the showman came in, pulling the tent flap across behind him. It was time for the fight to begin. The man disappeared momentarily behind the crowd, then reappeared with The Champ! Mary took one look at him and then at Bob Farhall, surrounded by his cheering mates. It would be like David facing Goliath, but this time there would be a different end to the story. In spite of his friends' enthusiastic cheering it was obvious Bob felt far from confident. Mary listened to the showman, who was also referee, shouting out the rules.
"If it gets too dangerous we stop the match," he croaked. "The referee's decision is final!"
Mary pressed her lips together, closed her eyes, put her fingers in her ears and stood behind Fred for the duration of the fight. It did not last long. After just two or three minutes there came a sickening thud which Mary could hear in spite of all attempts at shutting out the noise of the conflict. Bob's friends booed the champion boxer and hollered encouragement at Bob, who was sitting up and looking round him with a dazed expression. Eventually he tottered to his feet, but was too concussed and drunk to carry on fighting.
"Move along now," the showman began. "Hurry along. There'll be another match in ten minutes. Who'll be next to fight

now? Which gen'leman among you is brave enough to fight and win that guinea?"

Mary stumbled into the fresh air, desperate to escape. The evening was spoiled. She turned to look for Fred. She wanted him to walk her back to the Blacksmith's Arms where her family surely were by now. He did not appear. She pushed past the showman, who attempted to make her pay for entry. Fred was there, talking in a loud voice to Bob and his mates.

"Here's yer girl, Fred," said Bert, respectfully stepping aside.

"Mary!" Fred stepped across and put an arm round her. "Mary, I'm goin' to avenge poor Bob. I'm next to fight that so-called Champ. He won't be able to stand up to me."

Mary looked aghast.

"Don' worry Mary. I can lick any man. You ask them," looking backwards at the other men.

"Fred can knock anyone out," Bert agreed. "If anyone can get that guinea Fred can."

Mary was furious now. She felt hurt and neglected.

"Then I s'pose I'll have to make my own way back through the crowds."

"Tisn't far, Mary. Anyway, you could wait and see me win. If you don' wan' to watch you can step outside fer a minute or two as 't won't take long to finish him off."

"I don' want to see you fight. I don' want to see you at all ever."

Mary pushed out of the tent again and hurried round the edge of the fair, dodging through the crowds of reeling and noisy men. It was later than she had realized and there were few children or women around now. She ran the last few yards to the side gate of the inn and round to the kitchen entrance. The door was locked so she rapped frantically at it, glancing nervously behind her at the drunken youths shouting and lurching about just outside the gate.

The door flung open and her father stood there looking rather stern.

"Didn't think you was goin' to be out so long miss. I was

jest goin' to send out a search party." He peered behind her into the garden. "Where's young Carter? 'Spect he didn't want to show his face bringin' you back at this time. 'Tis gone eleven. The others are all gone home 'cept fer me and mother, so we'd best get the trap and be off ourselves."

Mary had arranged with her employers to stay the night at Soil Farm and return to Billingshurst next day, and she told her parents all about the evening's events as they drove home down the lane through the dark fields. The noise of the fair dwindled into the background as they left the lights behind them and were enveloped in the blackness of the September night.

****

Fred was scarcely aware of Mary's disappearance, being surrounded by friends and acquaintances – and some strangers too – loudly urging him on as preparations went ahead for the fight. He was being stripped of his jacket and best waistcoat, and automatically rolled up his shirt sleeves, unconsciously clenching and unclenching his fists as he did so. Someone pulled mufflers onto his hands and he punched the air with them, feeling great. He had lost sight of reality and his common sense had left him. In a mental haze induced by large quantities of ale, the heat inside the booth and the strong smell of sweat, pipe-smoke and beer, he abandoned himself to the aggression which arose within him, sending his pulse racing and his ego soaring.

"Goo fer it Fred," he heard Bert bawl in his ear at the last moment. "Smash 'is ugly face in!"

Fred waited in a corner of the ring. He was vaguely aware of the showman rattling off the rules, but was in no mood to take them in. A bell rang and Fred saw The Champ moving fast towards him. Instinctively his left fist shot out and caught the other man on the chin. Although more heavily built than Fred, the champion was no taller. Fred moved back and to one side, deft on his feet in spite of the excess alcohol in his blood, hearing the cheers of his supporters all around him. He felt a blow to his chin, which sent him staggering, but he quickly regained his balance as the cheers grew even louder.

The fight entered the fifth round, which was a record, for The Champ usually finished his opponents off in three rounds at the most. Fred sensed a slight tiredness in the other man. He had been fighting all evening and for several nights in a row, and even a champion must have his limits. Fred summoned up all his strength. He was determined to win this match.

In the third minute of the fifth round The Champ fell.

Fred waited for him to get up but he could only get as far as his knees, in spite of frantic urging from the referee.

The crowd went frantic with delight and began counting him out …..“nine, TEN!”, followed by a roar of triumph.

Fred raised his arms in the air and slowly turned round in a circle – there was scarcely a mark on him.

In a state of euphoria the crowd began to move off, anxious to slake their throats – dry with shouting and the smoky atmosphere – leaving just Bert to help Fred into his clothes again. Fred shrugged his arms into his jacket and looked about him. The Champ had been helped out by the irate booth-owner and another gypsy and only Bert and Fred wereleft in the tent.

Fred, who thought his anger had been spent, felt it rise up in him again.

"Wheer's that b----- villain gone?" He whirled round in a fury. "'e's cleared off wi'out givin' me my guinea the b------! 'E'll think twice 'bout that I tell 'ee."

Fred burst through the flap at the rear of the booth into what he presumed was The Champ's room, while Bert hovered anxiously inside the main part of the tent.

As he had suspected, Fred found a bloody cloth and some discarded clothes, but no sign of either The Champ or his boss.

He shoved his way out through another flap into the outside world, where the fair was gradually closing down. People were drifting off now and drunken shouts diminished into the distance as the revellers staggered home to their beds. Some of the stalls were already being dismantled.

    Fred grabbed onto the arm of a showman who was clearing up the freaks show.

    "Can yer tell us which of these vans belongs to the boxing man?"

    For a moment the gipsy, sensing his fellow traveller might be in some sort of trouble, was half-inclined to lie and say he had no idea which one it was, but something in the look of the young man holding tightly onto his arm urged him to tell the truth.

    "Just be'ind yer, Sir," he said, shaking his arm as Fred's grip loosened and he let it go.

    Fred did not bother to knock but burst into the van, where he was confronted by the showman's wife.

    "If yer want me 'usband 'e's not 'ere!" she said, without conviction.

    "Pardon me Missus," Fred replied, pushing past her.

    In the shadowy rear of the van the owner of the boxing booth was cowering. The Champ was sprawled out on a bed opposite him.

    "We got some unfinished business yer know," said Fred, deliberately striding the short length of the van and towering over the other man. The tankard the booth owner held in one hand shook slightly and for a minute he said nothing. Then, "Think again shepherd," he answered.

    "Where's that guinea, eh?" demanded Fred, pulling the other man to his feet by the scruff of his neck. "I won that guinea fair and square so where's it now then?"

    "You broke the rules," the man feebly protested.

    "What?" roared Fred, letting the showman fall back onto his seat.

    "I told yer at the outset – I am the referee and my word counts. I never counted The Champ out. The crowd shouted too fast and by my counting he WERE up by the count of ten!"

    "Gi' me my guinea you lyin' b------!"

    "You ain't gettin' any guinea so you better clear off before my friends help yer out."

Fred turned around and saw two other men had entered the van and were waiting menacingly by the door.

He turned and walked slowly up the van. The booth-owner rose and followed him, suddenly newly-confident, seeing he had the support of his fellow gypsies now.

"Sorry mate," he sneered, as Fred pushed past the men, who were waiting to see him leave. Suddenly Fred whirled round and punched the boxing booth owner in the face. With fists flying he punched to right and left, then ran down the steps and into the night, leaving men moaning and shouting behind him.

Fred slowed his pace and glanced back. No-one was following him. The gypsies he saw around him were busy with their own business. He was thirsty. There was no sign of Bert or any of his mates, but some late drinkers were still patronising the drinking booths. He went across and bought himself a drink with the last pennies in his pocket. One of the drinkers was known to him – a local man with whom he had never got on. There was no particular reason for this. They disliked one another, and although neither of them had ever said so to the other, they were both aware of it. Fred nodded at the man, who was sitting with a group of gypsies.

Two more gypsy men came over to join the group. They talked in quiet voices, glancing towards Fred and back at one another. Then the gypsies rose as one man and left Fred's acquaintance alone. He gave Fred a sideways look and fell to studying the dregs of his ale. Fred felt uneasy. He decided it was time to head for home. He walked purposefully away across the crushed grass of the green towards the lane, trying not to look behind him. At the point where the lane branched off, however, he paused and stared into the dark, listening carefully. He heard nothing to worry him, so set off at his usual steady pace.

Halfway down the lane which led to Soil Farm there was an oak tree. It was a landmark along the winding lane, as the hedges were kept low and there were few trees between Adversane and Soil. When the wind swept across, bringing driving rain, the tree was a place of shelter for farmworkers and people travelling to and from the scattered farm cottages. Fred always reckoned that tree was about a quarter of the way to Nobs Crook and tonight his eyes sought its familiar shape in the surrounding gloom. The distance to the tree seemed further than usual. Young and fit as he was, he had over-done it this evening, and his body yearned for rest! But he was feeling more sober with the passing minutes and beginning to re-evaluate the evening's events. He might have knocked out The Champ, but he had not got his guinea and – what was more – he didn't really care about all that now. It wasn't simply that he felt he had put the score right by punching the booth-owner. Again, that seemed unimportant. It was all a hollow victory. What had happened to his relationship with Mary was the question uppermost in his mind now. They had so few opportunities to see one another and both of them had been looking forward to this evening. She had looked so pretty and been so warm towards him. The evening had started out well. Then he had spoiled it all by getting himself involved in that fight. He remembered she was staying over-night at her family home, which was about three quarters of a mile from Nobs Crook. He would pass the farm on his way home, but she would be in her bed by now. He wondered if he might get up early and try to see her before she went back to her workplace.

His mind pre-occupied with these thoughts he walked on and was upon the oak tree before he realized it! As he walked past there was a sudden shout. He turned around and found himself facing a group of men. Before he could register what was happening they fell upon him. A cudgel slammed on his head, knocking him to the ground. A bottle smashed down on his forehead. He was not conscious as they beat him with sticks and broken beer bottles. It did not take them long to finish the job – so many on to one unarmed man. Quickly satisfied they cleared off. The young shepherd lay in a crumpled and bloody heap in the middle of the lane.

Fortunately Hezekiah drove Mary back via Soil Lane early next morning, so they were not aware of the discovery of Fred's body by the cowman from Jupps Farm until later that day. As they passed through Adversane they noticed how quickly the gypsies had taken down the rides, sideshows and booths. Many of the vans had gone already, including that of the boxing booth owner, although

Mary and her father would not have been aware of that! The hamlet was quiet – it being a Sunday morning, and a good many men nursing sore heads.

When news of the murder began to filter out the peaceful calm of Adversane was shattered. It took many years for the horror of the crime to fade from people's consciousness. Mary was beside herself with grief, but eventually the pain eased and five years later she married a farmer who was a regular customer of her employer. For years afterwards farmers who lived down Westlands Lane maintained they could not get their horses to take them past the oak tree late at night. It was known as Shepherd's Oak for the rest of its life, which was not a long one for an oak tree. In September 1958 it was struck by ball lightning and almost totally destroyed. Just a stump remains to mark the place where the shepherd's life was taken.

Chapter Four

After her first year at North Heath school Deborah's role changed from that of scholar to pupil teacher and she was given new responsibilities in the classroom. Older girls were regularly asked to clean Miss Dallimore's house, while the boys tidied her garden. Deborah's ambition to become a teacher and her natural talent for looking after the younger children meant she was usually excused from these onerous duties and told to help the smallest pupils with their lessons.

By the time they left school at twelve or thirteen years old all the girls were expected to be proficient needlewomen. At school they mended sheets and clothes for wealthy parishioners and Rev. Sinclair, or stitched shifts and shirts for the church to donate to the needy of the parish. The work was boring and the material hardwearing and difficult to sew. Often it would be spotted with dots of blood where the needles stabbed the small fingers attempting to push them through the stiff fabric. Deborah did not enjoy sewing at all, but knew it was an essential skill for a girl to acquire, so persevered. She preferred knitting, though knitting at school consisted of making blankets and socks for the charity box.

The boys, meanwhile, studied geography with Miss Dallimore, or spent time in the garden. On a sunny summer's day the girls took their handiwork outside. They often sent envious glances towards the boys, digging and planting as the girls stitched the heavy material. However, there were times when the boys toiled in the hot sunshine and envied the girls peacefully sewing in the shade!

Deborah's favourite lessons were composition writing, singing and scripture. The Rev. Sinclair visited the school most days and read Bible stories to the children. Each week the pupils had to memorise passages from the Bible to recite back to him the following week. These got increasingly long and complicated as the children grew older. Deborah had a good memory and looked forward to being asked, but most of the children loathed it and frequently got into trouble for stumbling or forgetting their piece.

Miss Dallimore stood by with her cane in one hand, which sent them into a worse state. She seldom used it, for she was a gentle soul beneath her severe outward appearance. There were occasions when the boys received a smart whack on the palm of the hand for laziness or insolence. The small children and the girls were never caned, but the fear of the punishment was always there.

While Deborah and her younger brothers enjoyed school, for the most part, John was eagerly waiting for the day when he would leave to begin work at the forge. In September 1862 he waved his siblings goodbye as they set off for school, and proudly followed Charles into the forge. Dick Harding's apprenticeship had run its course and he had moved away from Adversane, so Charles was glad to have his son's help.

In autumn 1864 Deborah left North Heath school for a position as an assistant teacher at Nutbourne. Miss Baker was now Head Mistress there, (or Governess, as she preferred to be addressed), and had moved home from Adversane to Pulborough. Charles bought his daughter her own pony and cart so she could drive herself to school and back.

"You be a young lady now," he told her. "You can't drag all the way to Nutbourne and work all day and there bain't another way to git there. I wun't have my darter, a school marm, lookin' a drazel ! That wouldn't be right."

For two and a half happy years Deborah worked alongside her old teacher. Life at work and home followed a pleasant and harmonious routine as the Puttocks enjoyed a period of calm and contentment. Deborah had already learned that such tranquil times are essentially transient and all the more precious because of it. When 1867 dawned none of the family was aware of the important events it would bring with it and the changes which would occur in a short space of time. By now all the children had left school. John continued to grow strong and skilful at his work in the forge. George worked for his uncle Philip at his nursery at Billingshurst and lodged with the family there. Tom lived in Horsham, where he was learning carpentry. The family was settled and the future was looking promising.

Grandmother Deborah was not her usual self that winter. She developed breathlessness and a hollow cough that would not go away and kept her awake at nights. She prided herself on "keeping on doing" and was as industrious as ever, rising early each morning and looking after her poultry and pigs, the house and the shop. Betsy Greenfield helped her in the shop and was a willing and bright assistant, but was young and flighty. Because Deborah was "done up for the winter" no-one noticed she was losing weight beneath her extra layers of clothes. Annie still lived-in and did much of the housework. She was the only person to notice a change in Deborah, but any remarks only elicited a curt reply from her mistress, "I'm orright Annie, stop worritin'."

In February Charles hurt his back during a tussle with a high-spirited horse. He decided to find another blacksmith to work with John in the forge and spend more time in the inn himself. In April Alfred Taylor began working for Charles. He had completed his apprenticeship at Maresfield and wanted to move further west to be nearer his relations. He received his bed and full board at the inn as part of his payment.

Alfred was twenty years old. He was strong and muscular, confident though rather quiet, friendly and good-looking, with brown curly hair, a neat moustache and blue eyes. He got on well with John and Charles was well pleased.

Preoccupied with his own health and the business of finding a replacement blacksmith diverted Charles' attention from other matters, and it was not until the onset of warm weather caused his mother to reluctantly shed some of her layers of clothes that Charles noticed how thin her arms had become. She moved slowly about her work.

"Mother, you'm lookin' dog-weary," Charles exclaimed, "and you be getting' thin as a bean-pole."

"Thank 'ee Charles," she replied disdainfully. "I likes to know I look so gant!"

"Now Mother, I be tryin' to help. I think you should see the doctor."

"Well, I don't. I jest feel a bit queasy that's all. There's nothin' I can't cure with my own herb tea."

Charles' daughter was as fond of her grandmother as ever, but she sometimes worked late at school and no longer had time to go round to Sayers each day. Alfred's presence was preoccupying her, too! Once she got home in the evening she was glad to accept his offer to unharness and feed the pony and put the cart away for her. It was not surprising that his good looks and thoughtful manner made Deborah's heart race faster than usual, while her grace and prettiness had a similar affect on him. One pleasant May afternoon they stood together by the pony and cart, deep in conversation, Deborah's laugh ringing through the still air.

Mary glanced shrewdly in their direction.

"Seems to me Alfred and Deborah looks like sweethearts standing so close together!" she observed to Charles.

"What's that?" He looked rather shocked.

"You must see Deborah's gigglesome and blushes wheniver she sees him."

"I doan't see what's the harm in that."

"Well then, s'posin' she weds Alfred Taylor. She can't be a school mistress then. Tisn't allowed fer married ladies to be teachers."

"Weds 'im? You be jumpin' ahead there, Mary. She'm still a maid and not thinkin' of weddin' Alfred or anyone else as yet."

"You see if I bain't right then Charlie," Mary answered, smiling knowingly as she continued darning.

Charles looked slightly anxious, but further reflection convinced him Deborah had no such ambitions. She had wanted to be a school teacher since she was a little girl and he was quite sure she had no intention of changing her plans. However, he kept an eye on the two of them. As the days passed even he could see Mary was right.

One day Alfred approached Charles looking uncharacteristically awkward and rather embarrassed.

"You got a problem Alf?" Charles asked, looking up from his ledger.

"No, Mr. Puttock. No problem. Well, I wouldn't say it was."

"What can I do for you then?" Charles asked rather testily. He did not want to be disturbed or distracted.

"I wanted to ask you somethin' Mr. Puttock."

"Well, ask away then Alfred."

Charles turned, folded his arms and looked directly at Alfred. He had a feeling he knew what was coming next!

"Er, I - I am hopin' you will agree ….."

"Agree to what?" Charles asked, with an unreasonable desire to increase the discomfiture of the younger man and postpone the asking of the question.

"Truth is, I loves Deborah and want your consent to marry her."

Charles glared at Alfred.

"Well, I ain't sure I wants to give it. Deborah's gettin' on well with her teachin'. I don' want 'er rushin' into anythin' like that."

"We wouldn't be gettin' wed yet, Mr. Puttock. I wants to be able to give Deborah a home of her own. If anythin' comes up fer rent we wants to take it. But we won' wed till we got a roof of our own and some furniture an' all."

"Well, I s'all think on it."

Charles deliberately turned his back towards Alfred and resumed staring at his ledger, though the numbers in it made even less sense than before to his disquieted brain.

As usual, Charles decided he needed to share this latest morsel of news with his mother and seek her opinion. She was picking currants in a desultory fashion, slowly filling her old trug basket. Again Charles was struck by how quickly she had aged in recent weeks.

"How are ye Mother?" he asked fondly.

"Middlin'," came the quick reply.

"Why doan' you git the gal to do that?"

"Because I like to do it myself, Charles!"

"I wanted to have a talk with you, if you got the time."

"Let's have a rest, then, Charles. Fer I will be honest, my legs are achey today."

The two of them sat on a garden seat surveying the blackcurrant bushes, which were laden with clusters of fruit as big as small grapes.

"I got some important news Mother. I jest had young Alfred Taylor round. He wants to wed our Deb'rah!"

"Oh yes." Deborah nodded sagely. "Can't say that's a surprise. I won' ask if she wants to wed him as you only have to look at them together to know it."

"I ain't asked her," Charles answered.

"Not asked her? Surely you should be talkin' to her 'bout it."

"I will, I will," Charles replied rather sulkily. "Thought I would see what you thinks fust."

"Well, if she loves him that's all there is to be said. I know she won' be able to carry on teaching, but she won' be getting' wed jus' yet will she? I knows she's always wanted to wed one day. She has always said so since she was a little maid."

"She 'asn't known 'im five minutes! And I thought maybe she'd do better than marry a blacksmith."

"Charles Puttock you be a fool. What's wrong with blacksmithing? For you of all people to say such a thing. A farrier, a blacksmith, whatever you want to call him, is a skilled craftsman. Besides, what matters most in a man is if he's a good, God-fearin' sort and I believe Alfred is. But I think it would be best if he moves into lodgin's for now. Tisn't right for them to be livin' under the same roof if they're promised to each other."

Maurice Harwood had taken over the family shoemaking business since the death of his father, Edward, and he and his wife wanted to let their spare room to a lodger to help make ends meet. So Charles suggested Alfred move in with them and take an increase in wages to compensate for his loss of bed and board at the inn.

"I'll be straight with ye Alfred. I doan't think it is a good idea for you to be livin' in the same house as our Deb'rah. It's not the right thing now you got engaged. She's bein' distracted from her teachin' and if you moves out it might help her settle down agen. She won't be eighteen 'til the autumn. She be too young to marry yet, and you got some savin' up to do first!"

So Alfred moved in with the Harwoods, but as they lived just the other side of the road, and the forge was next to the inn, Alfred and Deborah saw one another every day. Deborah seldom called in on her grandmother after school now. She was in a hurry to see Alfred as soon as possible. Once the meal had been eaten and chores dealt with, she spent some time brushing and re-pinning her long hair, listening out for Alfred's knock on the door.

Charles made a point of meeting her when she drove in one hot July afternoon.

"You had a good day maid?" he asked fondly.

"Yes – but a lot of children were out of school today, helping with hay harvest," she replied, climbing neatly down from the pony cart and quickly moving away.

"Deborah," her father called. She stopped and looked at him, noticing an urgent note in his voice.

"What is it?"

"Would you go and see your granny this evenin' please, instead of goin' off courtin' with Alfred. You hardly iver goes round there lately, and she could do with seein' you. You knows how fond she is of you. She don't seem quite herself and it would do her good."

Deborah felt a stab of remorse as her father's words sank in. She had flown in and out of Sayers of late when she went there at all, not stopping to chat as she had used to do, and had been neglecting her grandmother. So once the evening meal had been eaten and cleared away, Deborah followed the well-worn path through the grass that led from the inn to Sayers. Annie was alone in the kitchen.

"Your granny's gone up to her room already," she explained. "She's been goin' to bed early of late."

Deborah ran quietly upstairs and tapped her grandmother's bedroom door before opening it and peering in. It was a cloudy, thundery evening and the room faced away from the setting sun. Grandmother Deborah was sitting in a chair next to the window.

"Hello Deborah! It's nice to see you," she said gently.

"Are you alright?" Deborah asked anxiously, putting an arm around her grandmother's shoulders.

"Yes, yes, don' you worrit yourself," Grandmother replied gently, with a brave attempt at a smile. "Just thinkin' about things, that's all."

"What are you thinking about then?"

"Oh, this and that," Grandmother answered guardedly, gazing dreamily out of the window.

Deborah took her grandmother's hand and they sat together in the twilight watching the stars come out in the indigo sky. A thin sliver of new moon hung low above the horizon.

"A new moon through glass. That's unlucky," Deborah remarked, half jokingly.

"Now how could it be when it's such a lovely sight: like a glimpse of heaven."

"Let me close the shutters now and light the lamp Granny," Deborah urged, feeling increasingly uneasy. Grandmother never talked like that. She was always pragmatic and not given to fanciful notions. "Your hands feels like ice. Can I get you a hot drink before I go home?"

"No, no drink thank you my dear. An' don' worry 'bout lightin' the lamp for I think I'll soon get to bed. I feel weary tonight."

Now Deborah knew there was something wrong, for her grandmother seldom admitted to feeling tired or ill.

"I'll call in tomorrow before I leave for school," she said, leaning forward and dropping a kiss on the old woman's forehead. It felt cold and slightly damp.

"I look forward to it ...if you have the time. But don' worry too much. I know you are busy."

Deborah loitered in the doorway, reluctant to leave.

"D'you need a hand getting to bed or anything?"

The spark came back into her grandmother's eyes.

"No I don'. I'm quite capable of gettin' to bed," she snapped; then added, "thank you for asking, Deb."

Something made Deborah run back and give her

grandmother a hug, which was warmly returned. The two women clung together, and although neither spoke an understanding passed between them.

Tears poured down young Deborah's cheeks as she slipped into the inn and up to her room. She looked out of her window towards Sayers with an ache in her heart like a heavy weight, and she prayed to God to bless her grandmother and keep her safe. All night she tossed and turned and dreamed strange and disturbing dreams.

Next morning Deborah woke early from this restless sleep and hurried downstairs to visit Grandmother before breakfast. But before she reached the latch there was a hasty rapping at the door and there stood Annie, wringing her hands and sobbing uncontrollably.

Grandmother Deborah had died quietly and peacefully during the night, still sitting in her chair by the window.

****

Without its matriarchal figure Adversane was a poorer place. Deborah Puttock was missed by everybody – young and old. September came and a new school year, and the hot weather continued. In spite of the Indian summer, which bathed the hips and haws in mellow sunshine and kept the blackberries ripening later than usual, there remained a sombre atmosphere in the hamlet community. On a dismal day the sight of Mrs. Puttock's small but brisk person busily going about her everyday tasks had made them feel all was right with their world. Deborah had listened patiently to her neighbours' problems. Her knowledge of herbs had eased various ailments and injuries and her advice had been frequently sought, for many people could not afford doctors' fees. She had seen people into the world and watched over them when they left it, and she had seemed virtually indestructible.

Charles was aware of an enormous void in his life and felt unequal to making major decisions immediately after his mother's death. It was vital to keep the shop open for the people of Adversane, most of whom relied on it for their basic needs, so with the help of Annie and members of the family, Charles kept the shop going until a more permanent solution could be found.

Young Deborah went about her daily routine with a weight like a block of ice sitting deep down in her chest. All the while she was busy at school the weight lessened slightly, but was still there. The moment she took the horse's reins in her hands and set off down the lane towards home her tears flowed. As she wept, yellow and brown leaves fell silently onto her from the over-hanging branches, as if the trees shared her sorrow. The weeping seemed to melt the lump of ice within her, but left her exhausted and drained, and after a while the chill, heavy sensation returned.

Alfred tried to be there for her when she got home. It wrung his heart to see Deborah's drooping figure as she struggled to come to terms with her loss and he felt inadequate as he tried to ease her pain with small acts of support and kindness. However, his understanding and love helped Deborah through the first difficult months of her bereavement. Mary was a great help, too. She reminded Deborah of the courage and faith of her late grandmother.

"You was given your grandmother's name and you can't niver do better'n to follow 'er example," Mary said, wiping a tear from her own eye. "She were a good, Christian woman an' I come to love 'er a'most as if she were my own mother."

Deborah found a new closeness to her stepmother after her grandmother's death. Her father was strangely different. He gave her a turquoise ring which had belonged to his mother.

"She tol' me you were to 'ave it when 'er time came," he said gruffly, as Deborah looked at the dainty ring, resting in the palm of her hand. Although she had seen her grandmother wearing it many times, it looked different now, without its original owner. She slipped it on and saw how loose it was. On her grandmother's finger it had looked tight, shining brightly against the ageing, freckled skin. She supposed it had been loose on grandmother's finger when she had first worn it – a gift from Deborah's grandfather, who had died before she was born.

Although Charles and Deborah shared a common grief, she sensed her father was keeping something back. He seemed to be holding his grief close to himself, rather than opening up to her. She needed to be comforted by him, as she had been when her mother died over a decade earlier, but he was unapproachable.

Charles was going through a living hell. The loss of his adored mother, whom he had been used to see every day of his life, turned his world upside down. He lived in a daze; permanently tired and slightly the worse for drink much of the time. The thought of his daughter getting married in the near future brought no comfort. He could reconcile himself to her giving up teaching, but his secret fear was the thought of Deborah having children. When he saw Deborah he saw his first wife; small and fair and slightly delicate. He remembered the terrible day when Tommy was born and Mary was screaming in agony. He remembered the funeral, the crying, motherless children, the sickly new infant – destined to live such a short life - wailing night after night. Charles did not want that for his daughter. The death of his mother had brought all the pain of his earlier losses flooding back to him. Young Deborah meant the world to him. He could not bear to lose her, too.

What else is there to do once you have stopped reeling from the impact of tragedy but to gather up the broken pieces and start rebuilding? After a few months it got slightly easier for Charles to accept his mother had gone to her maker. He stopped drinking himself to sleep each night and went conscientiously about his work. He opened up to Mary about his fears for Deborah and she reassured him to some extent at least. "What will be, will be", Mary had said. "Havin' babies is allus a risk, but 'tis one most women is prepared to take, an' if Deb'rah chooses to wed and have childern 'tis but right an' nat'rel!"

It was decided to rent out the shop to John Peters from Pulborough. Hezekiah's son, also called John, lived in Sayers with his wife and family. He continued to help Hezekiah (now aged 71) to farm Soil and John and Charles looked after the land and livestock at Sayers.

In the spring of 1870 Deborah Puttock was married to Alfred

Taylor. They moved into Southlands Cottage, close to the inn. Mary Jane Taylor was born just over a year later, followed by Anne Rebecca in 1872. Charles fears proved groundless. Both children were strong and healthy and Deborah thrived on motherhood. It was a cruel irony that Charles never worried about his sons' welfare. He knew they had always been rather weak-chested, but they had reached manhood and were following their chosen trades. Then in the late winter of 1874 first Thomas and then George became ill, and returned to Adversane, being too sick to work. Mary and Annie cared for them and nursed them diligently, but in spite of the best efforts of Dr. Evershed and the two women, Thomas Puttock died in July 1874 at the age of 20, followed in October by George, aged 22.

When Deborah Taylor gave birth to a son in June, 1876, she named him Thomas Henry, after her two youngest brothers. Perhaps another son would have been named John George, but Tom was her only son. In October 1877 Ada Barbara was born, followed in February 1879 by Emma Maud.

Deborah and Alfred's family were a real comfort to Charles and Mary. Charles now realised his good fortune in having a married daughter with a family living close-by. Had Deborah decided to forego marriage and remain a school mistress, Charles would have had no grandchildren, for in January 1880 his only remaining son, John, died at the age of 28. He had never married and spent all his short life in Adversane, living at the inn and working in the forge.

This was a terrible shock to Charles. His own health began to fail and he was not well enough to continue working, so in 1881 Charles and Mary moved to Mare Hill to live with her elderly parents. Charles missed seeing his daughter and her family and found it difficult to settle, but eventually they all got used to the new situation, and there were frequent visits between Adversane and Pulborough. For the next few years life was uneventful. Charles and Mary's grandchildren grew up. The eldest two left school and found places as maids in local houses.

Then fate dealt what proved to be the final blow. In March 1887 Charles beloved daughter died in childbirth, aged thirty-seven. His old fear, which had been laid to rest by the successful births of

Deborah's five other children, proved to have been justified after all. Charles held his sorrow close to him, like a black cloak of mourning. Wrapped up in his grief, he took only the slightest notice of the rest of the world, going about its business just as if nothing had happened! There was something comforting for Charles in retreating back into the darkness which surrounded him, and not even Mary could reach him there.

Charles died in 1889 and was buried in Billingshurst churchyard, as his mother had been before him, and on the same date - 24th July.

Adversane about 1900

Chapter Five

On a warm September afternoon in 1894, Alice Humphrey was the centre of attention in the cottage of Haybourn, (pronounced Haybone), which is situated miles from any main road somewhere between Lee Place and North Heath. Fortunately Alice was a patient and sunny-natured girl and succumbed meekly to the washing and brushing and retying of ribbons by her excited sisters.

"Stand back," ordered their mother, admiring Alice's snow-white dress, stiff with starch and frothy with lace.

"She looks beautiful!" exclaimed Lotty, hopping from one foot to the other.

"You must stay like that now, Alice," ordered Ethel, who was the eldest and kept everyone else in check. "You got to look your best."

It was a special day, but not even Alice's parents and siblings knew just how special. How could they know that Alice would meet her future husband in a mere two hours time? Certainly Alice entertained no thoughts of that, for she was only just over a year old! The family were preparing to go to Adversane Fair where there was now a new annual event – a baby show! The Humphreys were quite sure Alice would win, with her rosy cheeks, glossy dark hair, green eyes and, most of all, her disarmingly placid and happy expression.

"She'll win, she'll win," shouted Fred, jumping over a stool and banging his elbow on the wall. "Ouch! She's the best baby."

"Settle down, Fred," said his mother, rather flustered as she straightened her hat. "You know there's really only one best baby an' every mother has it! Now come on, or we'll be late. We can go through the wood as it's been so dry."

They set off up the hot and dusty lane towards the wood, with Alice bouncing along in the wicker baby carriage, pushed by her brothers – Fred and Harry. There was always one sticky place in the middle of the wood, but they managed to get by without anyone getting mud on their best clothes.

"Stay close to me now," commanded Mrs. Humphrey, as the racket of the fair began to carry towards them across the meadows. She could see the excitement in her children's faces. "If you're good you can have some pennies to spend, but I haven't got many so you'd better spend 'em carefully!"

The baby show was one of the first events of the afternoon, so the family headed straight towards the inn, where it was to be held, the boys glancing back eagerly towards the more exciting attractions. But they were also interested in seeing the competition and, anyway, they knew better than to disobey their mother.

Alfred Taylor was outside the Blacksmith's Arms, setting up the spits to roast the sheep later on. His son, a thatcher, was helping him. Alfred saw little of his daughters, but he frequently saw Tom and had enlisted his help with the spits at the fair for the past few years. Tom was now eighteen years old and closely resembled his late mother, being small featured and quite fair, with blue eyes. Parents and children were converging with their babies and toddlers and Tom surveyed them rather nervously. He was not used to children and spent most of his time working alongside his employer, Mr. Sands.

The crowd grew and some of the babies got restless and began to cry, which in turn upset the others. Alice looked about her with equanimity and interest. There was so much colour and movement and noise. But she remained unruffled.

Then at last the judges arrived: Mr. and Mrs. Napper, Mr. and Mrs. Ireland and Mr. and Mrs. Hope, all resplendent in their best clothes.

The children were "shushed" and the babies given a last tidy-up; dribbly chins wiped dry and crumpled dresses tugged down.

There were three classes – under one, one to two and over two. Prizes were awarded in each category and an over-all winner would be chosen from all classes. As the Humphreys had hoped, Alice won the hearts of the judges and she was unanimously chosen as winner of the one to two age group. Finally the judges had to select the over-all winner. By this time the sound of crying babies and complaining children, added to the cacophony of the fair, was making it difficult for people to hear what the judges were saying.

"The over-all winner is Alice Humphrey," declared Mr. Hope in his loudest voice, all to no avail.

"Alice Humphrey," bawled Mr. Gillman, the landlord of the Blacksmith's Arms. "No-one can 'ear above this noise. Eh, Tom. You hold 'er up so everyone can see 'er! My 'ands is greasy. D'you mind if we 'old 'er up Missus Humphrey?"

Fanny Humphrey was pink with pleasure and embarrassment and nodded back at Mr. Gillman, thrusting the child into Tom Taylor's arms.

Tom had never held a baby in his arms since he was a small boy and had held his sisters, under strict supervision. He held Alice up to the crowd rather awkwardly, and she waved her little feet excitedly to and fro as they clapped and laughed. There were a number of disappointed faces, but most people took it in good part. Tom lowered Alice down to eye level and looked at her before passing her back to her mother. She was a very pretty baby, but in his wildest dreams he would not have believed that in eighteen years' time she would become his very pretty wife!

****

Alice Humphrey walked with her brothers and sisters down the long and winding lane to the main road and then on to North Heath when the time came for her to start school. After a few years the family moved to Marringdean Road, Billingshurst, but the children continued to walk to North Heath school each day, a distance of at least four miles. It was a long walk on a hot day and even longer when rain lashed down, there being little shade or shelter along the way. Sometimes they were lucky and got a lift on a cart or waggon at least part of the journey. It would have been nearly as long a walk for them to go to Billingshurst and the children accepted their daily trudge to and fro without complaint. "Shanks's pony" was the most usual way of getting around for the majority of people and the children's friends often had equally long walks over fields and along byways to reach school. They sometimes met up with Adversane children, also walking the comparatively short walk to North Heath. Amongst them were Henrietta and Arthur, whose father Eldred Evershed, was farm manager at Juppsland. They lived in a cottage down Westlands Lane, just beyond the notorious Shepherd's Oak. Alice was one of the "big girls" by this time, and enjoyed looking after the smaller children. Although they did not know it, the two families were to be closely linked together in years to come.

Every Friday the Humphrey's walk was helped along by the prospect of spending a farthing or two in the shop at Adversane. This thought helped them on their way to school when they discussed what to buy, and it sped them along the road homewards, when they would pause to get their few aniseed balls or fruit drops at Sayers. These would be sucked slowly the rest of the way home, for there was always a contest to see whose sweet lasted the longest!

The children were under strict instructions from Fanny to look carefully both ways down the railway line before crossing the tracks, even though the crossing-keeper closed the gates across the road before the trains passed through. On those occasions when their journey coincided with a train, Alice stood well back from the line, afraid of the speed and noise as it roared through.

Fred Humphrey – Alice's father – was a shepherd, so frequently spent days away living in his hut, especially during lambing. He was a quiet man, but had a twinkle in his eye. When he came home from the fields, a brace of dogs running ahead of him, the children ran to meet him. He teased them and made up little rhymes for them about their pets, and they loved to gather round him during those precious times he was with them all.

"Sing, Sing, you pretty young thing,
You'll be Freddy's wife when he gets you a ring…," Fred crooned to the cat, as it sat purring loudly on the arm of his chair, while the little girls giggled and begged him to "make up some more songs!"

Although they missed their father when he was sleeping away from home in the shepherd's hut out in the meadows, they never lost an opportunity to visit him there, and one of their regular duties was to take a turn at carrying food across the fields for him. Some of Alice's earliest memories were sitting on her mother's knee in a corner of the hut, looking about her at the assortment of tools essential for her father's work, all of which the children were strictly forbidden to touch. A large lantern hung by the door, where it could be quickly grabbed up by the shepherd if he heard a ewe in trouble during the night. Next to it was his crook and a broom. Shelves held an assortment of tins and bottles of medicines and lotions. In one corner there was a swaphook and a sharp clasp knife which her father used to dock the lambs' tails, trim hooves and cut sticks to make new crooks. (Alice kept well away from them. They were only slightly less frightening than the ferocious mantrap, which hung on the barn wall of a neighbouring farm!) In another corner of the hut was the shepherd's stove, with a kettle for Fred to make himself a drink and a saucepan for warming milk to feed orphan lambs. This was a job the children delighted to help with, when they got the chance.

When she was at home Alice had to help Fanny with the chores – as they all did. She worked hard for her mother, polishing and cleaning and preparing vegetables. At school she was a bright and conscientious little girl. When she reached the age of twelve she passed her school leaving exam and began working at Gratwicke House in Billingshurst, as a scullery maid.

Alice was not quite five feet tall and had to stand on a crate to reach the huge stone sink. For hours on end she stood there peeling and preparing vegetables, quietly crying with boredom and with longing for her home and family.

Eventually Alice adjusted to her work, there being little choice in the matter, living for her Sunday afternoons off, which were few and far between. She was promoted to kitchen maid after a year and a half, which meant she helped with the cooking – a better job than the unremitting drudgery of scullery maid, though the cook had a vicious temper.

While Alice was bravely getting on with her job, trying to stay on the right side of the cook and not think too much about what the family was doing at home, Tom Taylor was living a solitary life and carrying a burden of great sadness concealed within him.

Tom's father, Alfred, had always enjoyed a drink at the end of a long, hot day working in the forge. After his wife's death he spent an increasing amount of time in the Blacksmith's Arms. His two eldest daughters had already left home when Deborah died, and Ada and Emma, being only ten and eight years old, had gone to live with their grandparents. Tom stayed with his father until he left school, then moved in with his employers. By 1898 – the year Alice had started school – Tom's father's drinking and gambling problems had grown out of control. Alfred Taylor owed rent on his room at Adversane, owed money to the shop, the inn and the bookmakers. He had never faced up to the loss of his wife, preferring to drown out his grief with heavy drinking. There had been occasions when things improved for a time, usually as a result of the unconcealed distress Alfred read in his son's face. But the desperate yearning for a drink always returned. He drank himself into oblivion once again, eventually emerging into comparative normality. Then he roamed across the fields, lamenting his addiction and his loneliness.

Being threatened with eviction by his landlord, (who knew Alfred had spent his wages on drink rather than paying off his arrears), Alfred reeled out of the house and headed off towards Lordings Wood with his gun. He stumbled into the densest part of the wood, aimed the gun against his temple and pulled the trigger.

It was not until late in the evening that Alfred's landlord grew alarmed. What ever his condition, Alfred always came home. That night he did not. Next morning a search party set out, with Tom amongst them. Luckily Tom did not find his father's body, but it did not take long for others to discover Alfred, for locals knew his favourite walks.

After his father's death Tom became even quieter than before. He worked long hours, concentrating all his attention on the job in hand – harvesting and thatching. That summer he was often late back to Sands's cottage, where he ate the food which had been kept warm for him before falling into bed, exhausted by his long day's work. Sunday was his only free day and he spent most of it out walking. His mother and his school education had laid the foundations of a firm Christian belief, but it was in the countryside he felt closest to his maker, not inside a church. The woods and fields were his chief comforter and he felt his pain ease as he walked between the silent trees and along quiet lanes. As he walked his blue eyes sought every detail around him. He noticed song birds' nests in the hedges, sparrowhawks hovering overhead, the dusty green of the late summer foliage on the trees and ripening berries in the hedgerows. At night he gazed at the sky, inwardly naming the constellations and planets and looking out for shooting stars. He watched the moon wax and wane and the sun rise and set, silently taking mental notes and predicting the weather for the next few days. With a farmer's eye he noted the state of the land around him – good crops and poor crops, broken fences, good healthy stock and badly maintained hedges and ditches. Occasionally Tom visited his sisters, but he preferred his own company at this time. He enjoyed the occasional pint in the Blacksmith's Arms, but it took some time for him to return to the inn, which was full of reminders of the past. So Tom's life continued virtually unchanged for thirteen years and it seemed likely it would always be thus.

When she was visiting her family home at Marringdean Road, Alice occasionally saw Tom Taylor. He always lifted his hat to her and asked after her mother. She admired his good looks and polite manners, but he was a man in his thirties and she still only in her mid-teens so she paid little attention to him, although she pitied him for everyone knew about his father's suicide.

Then, the spring before her eighteenth birthday, Alice had a day's holiday at home. Gladys, the baby of the family, had not yet started school, and Alice took every opportunity she could find to spend time with her little sister and mother and help out with the chores.

It was a breezy spring morning of clear blue skies and fast scudding white clouds when Tom Taylor called at the cottage to take a look at the roof, which Fred had told him was leaking water through into the bedrooms.

As he walked up the garden path Tom heard the pleasant

sound of young voices singing, and discovered Alice hanging the family wash on the clothes line between the apple trees, while little Gladys carefully handed her the pegs. Alice was relishing the beauty of the spring morning and her holiday and she beamed at Tom with none of her customary shyness.

Tom had not seen Alice for several months and was surprised to find she had suddenly, or so it seemed, passed through childhood and become a young woman. He asked her if she would like a take a walk the following Sunday and she readily agreed. The weather remained warm and settled and Tom and Alice walked out together at every opportunity throughout that spring and summer.

Within a few weeks Tom had proposed, and Alice accepted his proposal without hesitation!

They married at West Chiltington church in April 1912, Alice travelling along the country lanes in a flower-bedecked pony trap, all the way from Marringdean. Tom had arranged for a photographer to record the occasion and the picture he took became a family heirloom. In the picture Tom looks much younger than his almost thirty-six years; perhaps because of his slim figure and small features. Alice is a slender, elegantly dressed girl, whose appealing large eyes gaze directly at the camera from beneath a wide-brimmed, flowery hat. Her kid-gloved left hand is slipped confidently through Tom's right arm, and he stands proudly by his young bride's side, immaculately dressed, with a glimpse of his silver watch chain visible across his neat waistcoat.

Tom and Alice began their married life in Chestnut Road, Billingshurst, while they waited to move into the new cottage they had arranged to rent at Kingslea Farm, Marringdean Lane. Alice passed her future home every time she visited her parents, and gazed in rapture at it. It was the one of two semi-detached cottages, each with a pointed gable, a big window facing a long garden and a substantial porch before the front door.

"I can't wait to move in," Alice exclaimed, as she discussed her future home with Fanny over a cup of tea. Then she cast her eyes down at her swelling figure,

"But I know I will have to wait a bit longer!"

At the end of February 1913 Alice gave birth to her first child – Ethel Mabel. Kingslea Cottage was ready soon after the birth, so once Alice's lying-in period was over and she was feeling fully recovered, the family was at last able to move into their new home.

Alice had inherited what remained of Tom's mother's possessions and Tom had been saving carefully during his bachelor years and was able to buy some fine pieces of furniture. In the front room were a solid mahogany table and chairs and some comfortable armchairs for the fireside. Alice and Fanny had made antimacassars for the backs of the chairs, using drawn-thread work to create patterned edges, and Alice embroidered cushions with sprays of roses and lilies. The room had a parquet floor, which was partly covered by a large woollen rug. Great-grandmother Deborah's china dogs sat on the mantel-piece next to a pair of green vases. A huge mirror hung above the fireplace, reflecting the oil painting on the opposite wall – a bowl of fruit and a folded cloth. The highly polished new table was kept covered with a velveteen cloth and a vase of flowers placed carefully in the centre. In the winter dried honesty and Chinese lanterns from Alice's garden took the place of fresh flowers. When the windows were open the scent of flowers wafted in from the borders just outside – wallflowers in the spring and stocks in the summer.

There was a cooking-range in the scullery and a copper for wash-day. Each morning before work Tom drew up bucket after bucket of water from the well in the back yard, to keep Alice supplied with enough water for cooking and washing and cleaning for the day. Alice had a big kitchen table with plenty of room for pastry making and preparing meat and vegetables. Above the table was another huge oil painting – this one was of the Aquitania. It was Tom's favourite picture and he sat and gazed at it as he ate his breakfast, fascinated by the frothy waves and wheeling gulls and the massive bulk of the ship. Although only twenty miles from the coast, people seldom saw the sea. It was a legendary place and the painting brought an air of adventure into the cosy seclusion of the scullery. Apart from breakfast, meals were usually eaten in the front room, the velveteen cloth being covered by a cotton one.

There was a short hall which led from the scullery to the front room on the right, the front door straight ahead and, to the left, the larder. Alice was delighted with the size of that. There were marble shelves which kept the dairy foods cool in the fiercest heat wave. All the food was fresh to begin with, the milk coming in straight from the milking-parlour, carried on a yoke by the dairy-maid (who was trailed by a string of farm-cats, waiting for their share of the milk). The cheese was made on the farm and the eggs collected almost as soon as they were laid. Tom quickly got to work on the garden and they were able to enjoy their own vegetables within a few weeks of moving in.

The porch was a small room in its own right! It was raised above ground level, so approached by three steps from the front path. Facing the door, there was the wall of the house on the left and a low wall on the right, the top of which had a broad wooden ledge – painted green to match the eaves and doors. The floor of the porch was paved with large terracotta tiles, protected by matting. On either side of the porch were small settles built into the fabric, with cushioned lids which lifted up, providing useful storage space. Here Alice kept her "Women's Weekly" magazines and, later on, the children's few outdoor toys – tops, balls and bats. The porch was an ideal place to air the baby and the capacious perambulator was put outside in all weathers, except fog, so Ethel could get plenty of healthy fresh air. She was sheltered from rain and wind in the snug porch and even in frosty weather would have her daily airing, a stone hot water bottle wrapped in flannel being placed at her little feet and layers of shawls and blankets around her.

Upstairs were three bedrooms. One looked out over the front gardens to the farmland on the other side of the lane. Another faced the back yard, where the shed and privy stood side by side before a line of ash and plum trees. In the middle of the yard was the well – with a stone roof smothered in honeysuckle and a small regiment of buckets nearby. The third bedroom overlooked the farmyard, just beyond a line of Mirabelle plum trees. The yard was always busy with chicken and bantams, dibbling, clucking and squawking or, on a hot day, simply snoozing in little hollows scooped out in the dust and scattered hay, blown out of the hay-loft. The farm buildings went back away from the yard and consisted of cow and milking sheds, a dairy, horse boxes for the hard-working carthorses and some pigsties. Back outside, the drive to the main farmhouse branched away from the yard to the right, while a gate to the left led into the cow pasture. Meadows stretched away into the distance, interspersed with little brakes of woodland and copses which were full of primroses, violets and bluebells in the spring.

Alice had never been happier. She was delighted with her home, which was greatly admired by her family and friends. She was even prouder of her baby daughter. The big pram had a linen lining which she frequently removed, washed and starched and then popped back into the pram. It was a miracle of white linen and broderie anglaise and little Ethel too always looked immaculate in stiff white dresses, trimmed with ribbons and lace. Alice regularly pushed her baby along the lane the short distance to her parents' cottage, where Ethel was fussed over and handed from mother to grandmother and back again.

Tom had never been happier either. Having reached his late thirties without finding a wife to share his life, he had begun to resign himself to a bachelor existence, lodging at the Sands' house. Now he had a beautiful wife and a baby, both of whom he adored. Tom and Alice were proud of their new home, where nearly every item had a fond memory attached to it. Tom's mother's and grandmother's carefully preserved ornaments and china were lovingly looked after, their own wedding presents equally cherished and cared for. He worked in his vegetable garden most days, always planning ahead for the next season, and seeking Alice's opinion on what he should plant. At the back of the shed he raised his own pigs, and kept some bantams nearby. Alice was a good cook and prepared substantial meals, with generous portions of their home-grown vegetables a part of the main course and puddings to follow. At tea-time there were boiled eggs, or a hunk of cheese with home-made pickle, jam or jelly and always cake she had baked herself. For the first time since he was a small boy, Tom was loved and looked after.

Alice, who had always been a pet in her family, continued to be fussed and loved by her husband. The age difference between them meant nothing. Only occasionally someone might remind them of their first meeting at Adversane Fair, and Tom smiled shyly while Alice giggled and blushed as the well-known story was aired yet again!

Alice & Tom's wedding, April 1912

Alice & baby Ethel

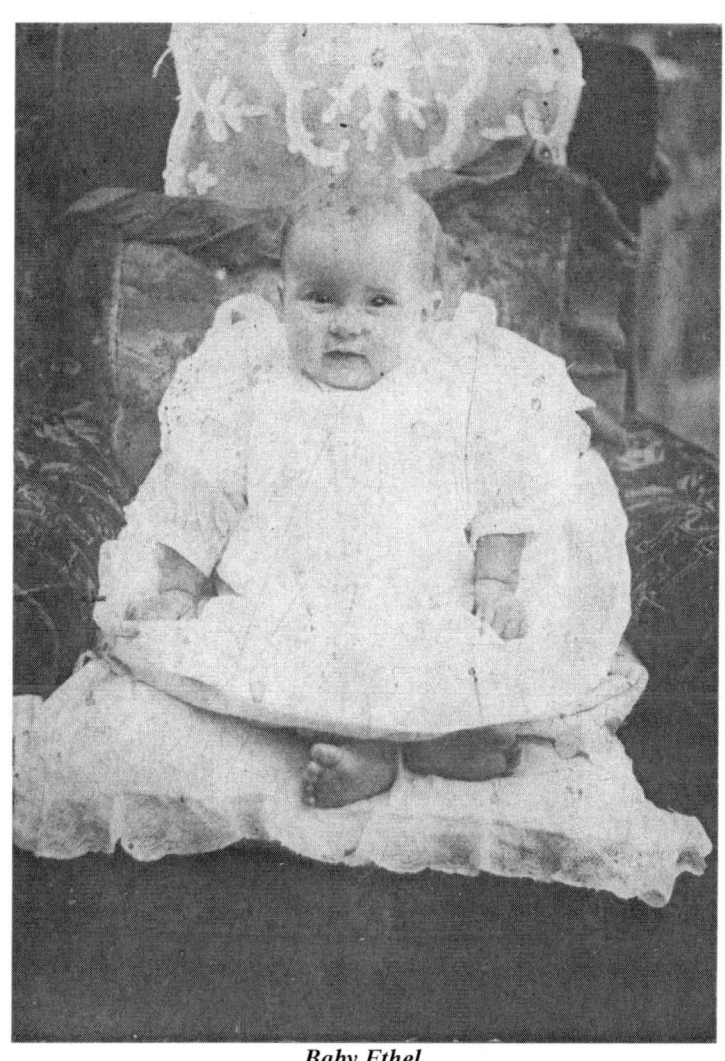

Baby Ethel

Chapter Six

The First World War began the year after Ethel's birth. Her father was too old to join the army, but Alice's older sister Ethel's husband, Uncle Jack, went to fight in the trenches. Their first child, Fred, was born a year to the day after Ethel. Tom agreed with Alice that his sister-in-law should not have to cope alone with her new baby, with her husband away fighting. So the household grew from three to five. In March, 1915 Alice gave birth to Stanley, followed by Thomas in 1917, so five increased to six and then to seven. To little Ethel, now four years old, it seemed as if the house would always be full of baby boys, with a continuous round of feeding and washing and changing going on. But the day eventually came when Aunt Ethel and baby Fred returned to Daux Road.

"Uncle Jack's coming back from the Front," Alice explained, as Ethel watched the two women packing baby clothes into a case. "So Auntie and Freddie are going home again!"

Ethel did not know what the Front was, but realized it was a bad place. By this time she had learned enough to know that men were fighting one another there and some of them grew sick or were badly hurt.

A few days after aunt and cousin left for their own home, Ethel came downstairs to find her mother bustling about with a nervous energy unusual with her.

"Help Stan get dressed and eat up your breakfast quickly, Ethel," Alice urged her, as she expertly pinned Tom into a clean nappy. "We're going to help Auntie. Uncle Jack got back last night and she needs a hand."

As Ethel helped her mother to push the pram, with Tom sleeping in one end and Stan chatting in the other, she wondered what Uncle Jack would be like. He had been living in a trench, shooting at Germans. She imagined a giant of a man with a gun in his hand. When they arrived at the familiar door she hung back slightly, peering behind her mother into the dim light of the kitchen.

"Come in and meet your Uncle Jack," Auntie Ethel urged,

pulling Ethel forward. "You don't remember him do you?"

Uncle Jack stood up slowly, rising from his chair by the fire. He was gaunt and thin and very white. He spoke softly to them in a voice which trembled slightly, then sat down again.

"I've put his uniform in the shed," Aunt Ethel said, "for it's far too dirty to have in the house."

While the baby slept in his pram, Stan and Ethel and their cousin Fred solemnly watched as Alice and Aunt Ethel took the big kitchen table outside. They covered it in an old blanket and then proceeded to iron Uncle Jack's uniform, going back and forth to the kitchen to take freshly heated irons off the top of the range. As the two women ironed the coarse material, Ethel could hear the popping sound of dying lice which had been infesting it.

Dinner was mince with mashed potatoes and carrots. Uncle Jack ate a small portion of mashed food, the same as Stanley and Fred, and his hand shook as he moved a fork very slowly to and from his mouth.

Later that week, Alice took her children with her on the weekly trip to Mr. Voice's grocery shop. As they waited with the pram by the railway crossing gates, a train drew into the station. Ethel looked up at the windows and saw nightmare faces before her: expressionless faces with blood-stained, bandaged heads and staring eyes or, worse still, no eyes at all, but more bandages above sunken, pallid cheeks and stubbly chins.

Ethel shrank behind her mother's skirts and waited for the train to move along.

Alice explained they were poor young men coming home from France, who had been injured in the fighting.

The memory of those wounded faces, eyes gazing at her but still seeing unimagined horrors, remained with Ethel for the rest of her life.

As Ethel grew older Tom told her about his mother, Deborah, and great-grandmother Deborah, whom he had never known but felt he had, for his own mother had spoken of her beloved grandmother so often.

"You rather favour my mother," Tom said. "She had a little

face like yours, but you've got your mother's brown hair."

"When I have a little girl I shall call her Deborah," Ethel firmly told her father, as she sat on his knee.

"Well, that would be nice," Tom smiled. "Now, you jump down a minute. I've somethin' to show you."

Tom left the kitchen and went upstairs, returning with a small box in his work-hardened hands. Carefully he opened the lid to reveal a ring – very thin and worn and with one blue stone missing.

"One day you will have this ring, Ethel," he said, gently lifting it from the satin cushion in which it rested. "It belonged to my mother and her grandmother before her. You shall have it when you get bigger."

Ethel held the ring in the palm of her small hand. She sensed the importance of the occasion and reverently handed it back to her father.

Ethel quickly learned that, as big sister, she was expected to help with the housework and looking after the babies. As soon as they were big enough to help with some small job or other, most children had daily chores to do. Although Ethel, as she grew older, felt she was expected to do more than her brothers, they too must see to their jobs before being allowed out to run wild in the fields and woods. While their sister peeled vegetables or mended socks, Stan and Tom would be polishing boots, carrying logs, feeding the hens or helping to clean out the pigsty.

Ethel's greatest friend was her Aunt Gladys, her mother's youngest sister, whom she saw on visits to Grandad and Granny Humphrey; (unless it was a school day, for Gladys was six years older than Ethel and so started school before her niece was born!) When she was free of school and chores, Gladys frequently ran along the road to visit her Aunt Alice and the baby. She was entrusted with the pram and proudly pushed Ethel up the road to her house or for a short walk in the other direction. Once Ethel's place as baby had been superseded by Stan, Gladys held the little girl's hand and toddled her along the road, or carried her in her arms, instead.

Once Ethel was big enough to manage the walk to

Billingshurst and back, the two girls often went shopping for their mothers.

"What shall we get with our penny Ethel?" Gladys asked one day, when they had some pocket money to spend. "Toffee lasts a nice long time."

Ethel agreed it should be toffee, so Gladys handed over the penny and got a slab of creamy toffee in return. Ethel watched as Gladys banged the slab against the edge of the wall to break it into pieces and then took the piece being held out to her.

"It's lovely," Ethel declared, as the two headed back up the road towards home. "Thank you Gladdy."

Overcome with affection, Gladys knelt down in front of Ethel, took her hands and looked into the small girl's face.

"I'll always be your best friend won't I Ethel?" she asked. "You will always be my best friend and I will be yours."

"You are my very best friend," Ethel solemnly agreed, and they hugged one another.

"Let's seal our friendship then," said Gladys eagerly. "To prove we will be best friends for ever, we will join ourselves together with a special thing – a bond!"

"What's that?" Ethel asked. "Like a skipping-rope?"

"No, we will glue ourselves together – with some of the toffee," Gladys announced. "Here."

She unwrapped what was left of the slab and they each licked it, then held it between their clasped hands. Thus united by the gluey toffee, they sauntered home to Kingslea, where Alice received a rather sticky shopping bag.

The bond of friendship never faltered and endured into old age, although, by then, Gladys and Ethel were living on opposite sides of the Atlantic.

****

When she was five years old Ethel caught measles and was very ill. It took her a long time to recover and she was slightly deaf for the next two years. She began attending a Sunday School in a church hall in Station Road, but was mortified when the stern gentleman who took the class mistook her deafness for inattention and informed the other children that Ethel Taylor was a wicked child! Such a child could not expect to go to heaven! When Alice discovered Ethel weeping copiously in anticipation of her Terrible Fate, she declared none of the children would go there again and sent them to the parish church Sunday School instead.

Because she had been so ill, Ethel was six years old before she began her education at Billingshurst Church of England school. What a long way from home it seemed - up Marringdean Road, past the station, past the imposing houses –Broomfield Lodge and Clevelands, (which her father told her had once belonged to the Puttocks), through the church meadows, up the flagstone path past Gratwicke House, (where her mother had once worked), and over the road to the school. Ethel was put in charge of some older children who lived nearby, but she did not know them very well and trailed miserably along behind them. Ethel's rather forlorn appearance drew the sympathy of one of the big girls – Evelyn Evershed – who already had charge of her own little brother, David. The Eversheds lived at Parbrook, but they looked out for Ethel and walked the last mile and a half to school with her. Ethel felt safe walking hand in hand with Evelyn, who had impressively long, thick black plaits, which swung sedately down her back, beautifully tied with enormous white ribbons. She was the younger sister of Henrietta and Arthur, who had walked to North Heath school with Ethel's mother over a decade earlier! The family had had to move to Parbrook when Mr. Hope, who owned Juppsland, knocked down their cottage at Adversane for the the valuable Horsham stone with which it had been roofed. After the Eversheds move to Parbrook, Eldred David, always known by his second name, was born on 23rd April, 1914.

During her first morning at school Ethel was taught how to do up boots with a button-hook, a skill she had already mastered at home thanks to the determined perseverance of her Aunt Ethel, who also taught her how to knit. Little Ethel had successfully knitted herself a pair of long socks for school and proudly wore them on her first day!

Much emphasis was put on handwriting lessons and from the moment they started school the children had to practice writing proper joined-up copperplate on their slates, just as Ethel's grandmother Deborah had had to do over sixty years before. So Ethel began the laborious business of learning to write on her first day.

In the afternoon the class began to learn "Hiawatha", repeating the lines after their teacher, Miss Webb, and reciting parrot-fashion, the small tongues somehow getting round the peculiar words – "Gitche Gumee" and "Nokomis". Ethel eagerly began her first reading book – not Peter and Jane, nor Janet and John but Fanny and Ned.

She quickly began to enjoy school, for she loved learning. Every lesson was a delight. She took satisfaction in producing neat sums and working out difficult problems. She loved writing stories and continued writing at home, reading the end results out to her small brothers at bedtime. Drawing was another favourite lesson, much preferred to sewing but something of a rarity for the girls, who were still expected to spend much of their school time learning to be skilful with a needle. Ethel did not often get drawing paper at home, so would use the borders of her father's newspaper, laboriously working away with a stub of a pencil. On one occasion she was drawing a picture of the baker's boy on a scrap of wrapping paper. He came to the back door as she put the finishing touches to her work and exclaimed, "Well I'm blessed. That's a picture of me you got there maid!" He was so taken with her drawing she gave it to him and he solemnly pocketed it with real delight.

Evelyn & David Evershed
Their faces reflect the long wait dressed in their
best for the photographer, who finally arrived after
they had changed back into their everyday clothes

"Buzzy" Wright was headmaster at Billingshurst school then – an irascible man, who relied on the cane to maintain order and wielded it with little provocation. If a child got a sum wrong there was a caning, not an explanation. When Ethel was in the Infants School he was a frightening figure of authority who ruled over the big boys and girls. She kept a respectful distance on the odd occasions she saw him, but most of the time she was safely under the wing of Miss Webb and the other mistresses. Once she went up to the Big School she soon had the sum of Buzzy Wright and did her best to stay on his right side. He was never angry with her, even when he saw her knitting under the desk! The girls were seldom caned anyway. They received lines instead. It was the boys who kept him busy with the cane. They deliberately antagonised him as only small boys know how, until he had them all lined up with their hands out in front of them. Then he went along the row, caning with as much zeal as he could muster. At the end of the line some cheeky child would enquire, "Does yer arm ache Sir?" and then he would proceed to cane them all over again!

There were times when the children winced at the unfair discipline. One family, who came from a farm just up the road beyond the Taylors, often arrived late. This was because their mother had died and they had to help their father with jobs round the farm before coming to school. They were thin and poorly looking children. In winter their hands were sore with chilblains and chapped with the cold, but they still had a whack on the palms of their hands to reprimand them for their late arrival.

By the time she was nine Ethel had both Stan and Tom to walk to school with her, as well as other children from Marringdean Road. They did not have bags full of homework like children do today, but they did carry their packed lunches. In winter these were quite substantial. Alice firmly believed an army marches on its stomach, and in very cold weather her small army of children were kept going with homemade pasties or potatoes for baking. These were entrusted to Ethel, who placed the potatoes on the hot stove in a corner of the classroom, making sure each one had its owner's initial scratched on it to avoid confusion with other children's! As the morning's lessons progressed the smell of cooking potatoes made the children increasingly desperate for their dinners! When not too heavily laden the children bowled their hoops along the road, which sped them to school in record time. There were regular seasons for different toys then. Spring was the time for marbles, tops and skipping. Summer was for two-ball (the girls) and cricket (mostly boys). In winter the girls collected in corners of the lobby to play jacks, while the boys flipped their cigarette cards and tried to add to their collections. Singing and circle games were popular with both sexes in the infants school, especially "What's the Time Mr. Wolf" and "Grandmother's Footsteps", but the older boys quickly dropped those pastimes for football and chasing as they grew older. The big girls still liked to play the singing games, and passed on the words and actions to the little ones: "The Big Ship Sails on the Alley-alley-oh", "Poor Sally Sits A-Weeping", "Queenie, Queenie, Who's Got the Ball" and "In and Out the Dusky Bluebells".

Probably the worst thing to happen to Ethel during her time at school was her first visit to a dentist! The children walked in crocodile down the slopes of the Bowling Alley, (not easy going down the steeply sloping hillside which led from the school), and along the path to the village hall, where a primitive dental surgery had been set up in one of the back rooms. After an inspection some unfortunate ones were given letters to take back home, informing the parents that their child needed some treatment. When Ethel was ten she was the recipient of one of those dreaded letters and reluctantly took it home, her fingers burning to pull it out of her bag and push it away into the bushes. However, she gave it to Alice who decided to allow the school dentist to extract one of Ethel's back teeth – a milk tooth, but a molar right at the back of her mouth.

A couple of weeks later the dentist returned to the hall and Ethel was among the children escorted to that dreadful back room. How different the Bowling Alley seemed that day as they walked towards their doom. The bracken was dull, the flowers hung their heads and there was no thrill to be had from descending the steep slopes from the school to the path at the bottom, (usually a joyful scramble!)

When Ethel's name was called she entered the room tremblingly and looked at the dreaded throne-like chair.

"Ah, sit down, sit down," the dentist urged her, frowning at her through small spectacles. Ethel climbed onto the leather seat, where she sat bolt upright, watching the dentist and his nurse as they sorted out the necessary instruments of torture. One glimpse of those was enough. Ethel jumped out of the chair and ran quietly out of the door, out of the village hall and up the High Street as quickly as she could, not daring to glance behind her. She dodged between gossiping villagers outside the shops and ran faster than she had ever run in her life before. Pausing for breath on the flagstone path that led to the church, she risked a glance behind her, and was greatly relieved to find the dentist and his nurse were not reaching out to grab her as she had feared. Though there was no sign of them she did not pause for long but continued running all the way home. Once there she fell on the back door, but it was locked and the house shut up. Her mother had gone shopping. What should she do? Ethel found a lump of chalk in the garden, which her mother used to whiten the step. Quickly she wrote "BEWARE OF THE DOG" on the lavatory door, then dodged inside and bolted it shut. Peering through a crack in the door she waited for the arrival of the dentist, but after what seemed an eternity it was the comforting sight of her mother which greeted her eyes as she returned from her shopping trip, with Mollie in the pram.

Unfortunately for Ethel, her appointment with the dentist was only delayed by a day. Next morning she had to mount the dreaded chair again and waited in trepidation for some reprimand from the dentist. However, he did not say a word, but he did keep his eyes firmly fixed on his patient.

There was another traumatic occasion for Ethel when she was called from her lessons to the staff room, where her brother Tom was writhing in agony with a broken leg. Still covered in mud from the football pitch, he cried and squirmed on a stretcher, while the doctor endeavoured to examine his leg. Ethel's hand in his was the only anaesthetic he would receive while his leg was put in splints. She screwed her eyes up in sympathy and squeezed the hand which grasped hers. How long could this go on for? Eventually the doctor was satisfied. By this time Bert Gray's cart had arrived, bringing Bert and Tom Senior, so young Tom was carried on his stretcher and lifted onto the cart. With his father and Ethel either side of him, Tom progressed slowly back home. Dr. Venables drove his gig along behind the cart to Kingslea and supervised Tom's installation on the sofa in the front room. Having given Alice a list of instructions and a promise to call next day, the doctor drove away, leaving Tom resting grandly on the big sofa! For six weeks he reigned over the house, while the family petted him, waited on him and did all they could to spoil him. Once the leg was healed it was as straight and strong as if it had never been broken – a testimony to the skill of the G.P.

****

Most of the time school followed a very distinct routine, with little to vary the day to day pattern of lessons. However, there were diversions throughout the year, which were beacons of light to brighten the dull curriculum.

Few children at Billingshurst school had either seen or heard a wireless set. The wireless was beyond the means of most families, so it was an important and significant moment in their lives when Mr. Wright informed them that the schoolchildren, and their parents, were invited to the Womens Hall to listen to the commentary of the University Boat Race. Probably nothing they had ever done in their short lives had been as exciting as this! The day before the race they were allowed to spend the afternoon making paper rosettes, which they painted either dark or light blue, to show where their loyalties lay.

Ethel was one of the lucky few who had already experienced the wonder of the wireless! One bright sunny day during the school holidays, Alice had announced that she was taking the children to visit her sister, their Auntie Madge, who had recently moved to

Adversane. Mollie was a tiny baby, so Ethel, Stan and Tom took turns to help their mother push the pram up Beke Hill, along the Marringdean road to Steep Wood, then right and straight up the long road to Adversane. It was a peaceful route, with only the occasional horseman or farm waggon to disturb the dust. The blackberries were starting to ripen and crab apples and hips and haws just showing a hint of rose.

They crossed the level crossing with care, the children looking hopefully up and down to see if a train was imminent, then continued the short distance to the crossroads. They didn't often go to Adversane, apart from a visit to the fair in September, for there was nothing to take them there. As Ethel walked next to the pram she looked around her. In front of her was the green, where ducks were dozing at the edge of the small pond. The other side of the road was the Blacksmith's Arms, which she knew had been her grandmother's home, and the house adjacent to the smithy had been her great-great-grandmother's house. Tom had told her about them in some detail. She tried to imagine her unknown grandmother as a little girl, running around on the grass with a hoop or a ball, a girl with no mother to look after her.

They turned sharp left to follow a brick path along the front of the malthouse, which was a malthouse no longer, but a series of small cottages. Ethel counted the numbers on the doors, starting at 7 and going backwards. In between the doors she noted the enormous slabs of sandstone which made the wall almost golden in the summer sun. Against the walls apples and pears were beginning to ripen in the hot sunshine. Alice stopped outside number 4 and let Stan knock the door. Tom pushed his finger into a small hole in the warm stone, and particles crumbled onto the path. His mother barely had time to reprimand him before the door swung open and Auntie Madge stood beaming at them.

They stepped into a narrow hall, then through a door into the living room, which had a gutter running through it, a relic of the years when the building was still a malthouse and hops had been washed here. The children amused themselves hopping in and out of the gutter while Madge admired the new baby as she helped her sister bring the pram into the hall.

"I thought the boys would be tired after that hot walk," Alice exclaimed. "Sit still now and quieten down, or you'll wake Mollie up."

The children obediently sat down in a neat line on their Aunt's settee.

"What's that?" Tom suddenly asked, indicating a strange object on the dining table. It had wires leading from it to what appeared to be rather clumsy ear-muffs.

"I know what it is," Ethel and Stan shouted in chorus.

"It's a crystal set!" Stan concluded.

"Can we listen to it?" Ethel asked, fidgeting with excitement.

Aunt Madge smiled proudly.

"I should think you might! Now, I'm just going to make us a drink, as your mum must be thirsty after walking round here on such a hot day, and then you can listen in," she told them, disappearing into the small scullery. Ethel followed and watched as her aunt made drinks and put some cakes on a plate. She could scarcely contain her excitement and impatience as Aunt Madge put fresh milk in the jug and a cross-stitched tea-cosy over the pot.

"You bring the cakes, Ethel, and then we can settle down."

Ethel obediently followed her aunt back into the cool living room, where the boys were leaning across the table, squinting at the wireless, quite fascinated by the hidden potential of this small and alien machine. Ethel did "eeny, meeny, miny mo!" to see which of the three children could have first listen in. The boys were first, but she didn't mind waiting – for a minute or two at least! Madge and Alice sipped their tea and smiled at the expressions on the boys' faces.

"You should get one, Alice, they have some lovely music," Madge said, and Alice and Ethel took a turn with the headphones.

Ethel listened enraptured to the warbling voice of a soprano. What made this magic happen, she wondered. How could you hear someone singing miles and miles away. It was absolutely amazing.

The children talked of nothing else but the wireless set all the way home.

"We'll see," Tom said, when they pleaded with him to buy one. Tom was not particularly interested in modern inventions and it would take several years before he gave into pressure from his family and invested in a wireless set. Then, of course, he spent as much time as he could seated with his best ear next to the set, for his hearing was beginning to go.

Another innovation which brightened school life was the invention of the crossword puzzle. Every Friday afternoon a puzzle was carefully reproduced on the blackboard for the class to solve between them. Children were selected to read the questions and arms shot up into the air as they vied to give the answers! It made a refreshing change from the usual spelling and grammar lessons.

The 24th May was Empire Day and lessons were abandoned. The children were exceptionally bright and clean that morning – the boys with their boots well polished and faces scrubbed and the girls in white dresses and starched pinafores, most carrying bunches of marguerite daisies with which to decorate the school. Some of the older children had been selected already to represent different Commonwealth countries, and had special costumes to wear. One especially favoured older girl would be Britannia, enthroned on the school stage, with her attendants about her.

This was one of the rare occasions when parents came to the school. The morning's entertainment of recitations, songs and dances was much appreciated by those who were able to come and watch, but the highlight of the day, for most of the children, was the announcement of a half day holiday!

Being a church school, the children filed down to St. Mary's at intervals throughout the ecumenical year, to attend special services. On Ash Wednesday they took twigs from ash trees to school and had to keep them handy until mid-day, or otherwise they were likely to receive a pinch and a punch! After noon had passed they were all safe! Just as no-one could play an April Fool trick after twelve noon on All Fools Day, neither could they pinch a twigless child after noon on Ash Wednesday! Before that magic hour you had to be wary. Even in the solemn atmosphere of the church it was wise

to show your ash twig to any child in your pew who looked the slightest bit menacing.
A pinch and a punch was also the penalty you received for not keeping your fingers crossed on the first day of each month. If another child began, "Pinch, punch the first day of the month", you had to swiftly hold up two crossed fingers in self-defence!
Harvest thanksgiving was one of the major celebrations in school, church and at home, for this was a time when most people around the area were either involved in farming or preparing food or growing their own vegetables and fruit.
Christmas was celebrated at school, although in a quieter way than it is now. The children made decorations to hang around the classrooms and practiced carols for the Christmas concert. There were party games in the afternoon on the last day, however, and Miss Webb gave all her pupils an orange to take home.

****

Ethel was a motherly child and as she grew older often had a group of children in tow – taking them to school, or shopping or for a walk. She not only "minded" her brothers and sister, but neighbours' children. Not only children were placed in her care, but babies too!
One late afternoon Tom came into the kitchen carefully carrying a small bundle. He grinned at Ethel as she jumped up and ran over to him.
"What've you got Dad?" she asked, trying to see inside the bundle of sacking.
"I've got a baby for you to look after Ethel," her father announced, giving Alice a sideways glance to see her reaction!
"Ah, it's lovely," Ethel exclaimed, parting the folds of the sack to reveal a tiny piglet. Tenderly she took the little runt and gazed rapturously at its wrinkled face.
During her childhood she received several weak and sickly piglets to raise. She lavished love and attention on them,

conscientiously getting up in the night to feed them with bottles of warmed milk, changing their bedding and pushing them around in her dolls pram. When Ethel was at school Alice gave the piglets their feeds. On one occasion she went to visit her parents with a baby at one end of the pram and a piglet tucked up at the other end, much to the surprise of a lady who stopped to admire the baby!

As they grew bigger the pigs became too lively to remain living in the house, so were sent back to the sty. However, they remained affectionate and friendly and the children lured them back indoors whenever they could. On one occasion a favourite pig was lying asleep under the scullery table, unbeknown to Alice, who proceeded to lay the table ready for dinner. Just as she was setting the food down the pig stood up, the table lurched to one side and the food, crockery and cutlery slid down onto the floor. The pig was banished from then on and the children had a good talking-to!

Inevitably these happy days of bringing up the pigs were short-lived. There was always a fateful day when Ethel came home from school to find her adopted baby had been slaughtered. Tears were shed in plenty, but there was always another ailing piglet to take the place of the one which had gone, and she had to admit to herself that the pigs had a very happy life, if a short one.

As she grew older Ethel's workload increased. On Saturday mornings she walked up the road to her grandmother's house to help with the housework. In return for polishing the brass and silver, Grandmother gave her a huge bread pudding to take home, which she carried carefully back up the road, the heavy enamel dish making her small arms ache.

Tom Taylor was renowned for his accuracy as a weather forecaster. Farmers from around the area dropped by as harvest time approached, to ask his opinion on the weather.

"Call back in the mornin' and I'll tell you," he would say.

That evening he would go outside and look at the sun-set, consider the rising moon, the mist, the wind direction, gaze at the constellations as the sky darkened. Next morning he went through a similar procedure. When the farmers called, anxious to know if they could start harvesting, he would either reassure or warn them. He never failed to get it right.

Ethel loved to go star-gazing with her father on frosty winter nights. He pointed out the constellations to her and told her about shooting stars, comets and the phases of the moon. It was an awesome mystery – the vastness of that huge dome of sky sparkling with thousands of stars. She was glad to have the comforting presence of her father next to her; reassuringly, humanly warm.

Hay and wheat harvest were times when everybody lent a hand if they could. Toiling in the hot sun was no hardship for young Ethel, who cheerfully helped to build the stooks or the haystacks. She sometimes worked on top of the stacks, smoothing the hay as it was tossed aloft. Picnics in the hay-fields were a delight, but the greatest joy of all was riding back to the yard on the hay or – better still – on the back of one of the cart horses. On sizzling summer days even the horses wore hats to shield them from the sun's rays. Farmer Gray always held a Harvest Supper in September, to which everyone was invited.

With the harvest in and the larder well-stocked the prospect of winter was not really daunting. Alice and Ethel had salted, pickled, bottled, dried and preserved as many vegetables and as much fruit as time and availability would permit. The children had picked pounds of blackberries and crab apples from the hedgerows to add to the home-grown foods. During the damp autumn days there was plenty to eat for mushrooms were plentiful in fields regularly manured by the horses and most people had a selection of fruit trees and a vegetable plot to harvest. The shelves of the shed and even bedroom window ledges at Kingslea were covered in neat rows of apples and pears, spread on newspaper, which gradually disappeared as pies and puddings were made during the following months. Rabbits were a real menace in the countryside and garden and had to be controlled, so they frequently ended up on the dinner-table, either roast or in a casserole.

The children were well fed, which was not always the case in those days. Coming in from school on a summer's day, there was always a pail of cold milk in the larder which they were invited to dip their mugs into as often as they wanted. Sometimes Alice made lemonade or ginger beer for a special treat. The fishman travelled up by train from Littlehampton each week and pushed his barrow along the road, calling at those houses where he knew he would get custom. Alice bought fresh herrings and sprats. The distinctive smell and homely sizzle of fish in the pan was a welcome greeting as the hungry children stumbled in the door on a chilly autumn afternoon. Though Alice made most of the cakes they ate, she bought bread and buns from the baker boy when he called, and muffins from the muffin man, whose approach was heralded by the sound of his bell echoing round the farmyard.

Alice relied increasingly on Ethel's proficiency with housework, for she suffered several miscarriages between the birth of Tom and Mollie, who was born in May, 1923. The midwife helped look after the other children then, for several days during Alice's lying-in, but Ethel could cope marvellously well without her. However, Ethel's absence from school was noted and an attendance officer called. This was shameful to Ethel, but she was relieved as well for she did not like falling behind with her school-work. Being a bright girl, she quickly caught up and continued to learn even as she knitted clothes for her siblings under the cover of the desk lid!

Many of Ethel's jobs were not really chores at all. She loved to help her father in the garden, collecting the pearly white new potatoes as he carefully dug them out of the ground, or meticulously sowing rows of radish and lettuce seed in the drills he prepared. She enjoyed preparing the fresh vegetables for her mother to cook, sitting on the sunny back step with a basket of broad beans or peas to shell or a basin of currants to prepare for jam-making. On winter mornings the kitchen was a cosy place to be, making currant buns or jam tarts. In the evenings the family sometimes worked together at the table, making rag rugs; taking turns at cutting the cloth up into strips and weaving it in and out of the sacking with a special hook.

When she reached the age of eleven her mother began to teach Ethel new skills: how to skin and prepare a rabbit and how to pluck a fowl. Ethel's fingers grew sore with picking at the resisting stubs of feathers. When she had got out as many feathers as she could, she scorched the stubble with a candle flame to help remove the obstinate few remaining. But this was not such an unpleasant job as gutting the rabbits and poultry! Compared with Stan Ethel got off lightly. He had been taught how to wring the necks of the chickens she prepared for the table, and had to assist his father with slaughtering their pigs.

About this time, Tom – now approaching fifty - developed cataracts in both eyes and went to a Brighton hospital to have them removed. In those days this meant a three week stay. When he eventually returned home Ethel was the one who put drops in his eyes every day, sitting on his knee to make it easier to reach! She read the paper to him, the Bible, library books and even the boys' comics. Tom was unable to go back to work for some time and was told to rest at home. This was a tall order for someone used to being outdoors during most of the daylight hours. The weather was cold and often raining, but he still needed his exercise. Alice kept bumping into him as she went about her housework, for he insisted on walking up and down and round the house for half an hour at a time.

"I go to the larder and collide with him coming out again," she complained to her sister, "and then I go to fetch something from the front room and meet him coming through the door. It will be a relief to everybody when he can get back to work!"

Sunday was a special day. The children were all expected to go to church and the boys were in the choir. They also all had a turn at pumping up the organ for the hymn singing, which was quite hard work, but earned them some useful pocket money. In the afternoon most people changed into their best clothes and visited relatives, or were visited, or simply went for a walk. On summer Sundays the Taylor family often roamed over the fields to Andrews Hill and back down to Parbrook, stopping to buy chocolate and peppermints at the Tucker's shop before making their way home along the road.

Home life then, as now, was brightened by regular festivals and treats.

Shrove Tuesday was Pancake Day, and Alice made a huge bowl of batter to satisfy the appetites of her growing family.

Good Friday was a thoughtful and rather sad day. The

children went to church. They were well instructed in the Bible and knew the full story of the crucifixion and the significance of Good Friday. Ethel sat on the back door-step at Kingslea and sorrowfully ate her Hot Cross Bun, feeling guilty because it tasted so delicious, yet was a reminder of the Cross. Should she really be enjoying it that much?

At home Tom sowed his new potatoes. They must always be sown on Good Friday he told Ethel, to avoid getting blackfly later on.

But Easter Sunday was joyous. The church and the house were filled with spring flowers, catkins and greenery. After church there was a special roast lunch and relations came to visit or were visited. If it was a fine day they all walked over the fields to enjoy the carpets of primroses and wood anemones, (which they called windflowers). Alice made a big fruit cake for tea and there were hard-boiled eggs to draw faces on. Tom bought little bars of chocolate for the children.

The Sunday School outing to the seaside was the big event of the summer, for most children attended one Sunday School or other. The Chapel was said to have the best outings, but which ever church the children attended there was always a summer treat for all the family. A visit to the coast was usually taken by train to Littlehampton, but sometimes a charabanc would be hired to take the excited children and equally excited parents to the misty realms beyond the distant Downs. It was worlds apart from their familiar surroundings of field and wood. It was an alien place full of adventure and surprises – the strange salty smell, the odd sensation of walking on the cold, wet sandy ridges, the weird strands of weed which expanded into delicate red lace when floated in the water. Once Ethel walked all alone away from the crowd on the beach, following the water as it receded. On and on she walked, her eyes fixed on the horizon. Soon she must see France, surely. She did not look back, because she knew if she did she would want to turn around and run to safety. The desire for adventure was strong, so she walked on, pausing occasionally to examine a shell, a winkle or a little crab scuttling over the sand. Still the water moved away from

England to France. She must keep walking so she could tell everyone she had seen France. It must come into view soon. Then the silence struck her. It was so quiet and still. She turned about and looked behind her. The shore was a line peopled with little dots. One of those dots was her mother. She would be worried! It seemed as if France was going to have to wait after all. Once she began to walk back, panic set in. Suppose the tide turned and flowed in fast. She couldn't swim. She would drown. Ethel ran and ran, stubbing her bare toes on sharp rocks and slipping over wet seaweed. When she finally got to the dry sand she found herself several breakwaters away from the church party. Inevitably, she was in for a scolding, but she did not mind at all. She was still the happy recipient of a stick of rock, which she slowly and sleepily sucked all the way home.

The other main event of the summer was the Flower Show, held in August. The children at Billingshurst School prepared craft work and drawings at school throughout the summer term which were entered into the show. The Taylors were among those who made things at home as well. Ethel's chief delight lay in making a nosegay of wildflowers. She never tired of picking flowers and carefully arranged them to best effect.

On the morning of the show the family joined the trickle of people making their way to the big marquee, usually at Summers Place, bearing baskets of fruit and vegetables, home-made wine, honey and flowers. Entries had to be in place by 8.30 am, and the early morning air was sweet with the scent of the produce mingling with the crushed grass, still wet with dew.

During the morning the judges deliberated over the entries, slicing and prodding and tasting and then awarding the prizes. The show opened to the public at 3.00 p.m., so the children were in an agony of waiting as the day crawled by. At last they were all ready in their second-best clothes and hurried along in the summer heat towards the show. The very first thing to be done, of course, was see if any of the family had succeeded in winning a prize. What joy to find a green, blue or – best of all – red label, indicating a prize. A Highly Commended was good, but not as good as winning a few precious pennies!

After a thorough tour of the marquee, frequently interrupted by pauses to talk to old friends, an announcement would be made through the megaphone that the races would be commencing at 4.30, so there began a general drift towards the racing area. There were races for children and adults, beginning with novelty races for the little ones.

It seemed a long walk back up Marringdean Road after the excitement of the afternoon and the children were glad to get into their beds. Soon the summer would be over and they would be back at school, but for now their minds were busy spending the extra pennies they had won at the Flower Show.

The family usually went to Adversane Fair in September, where Tom continued to help with erecting the spit for the roasts. Every year Alice told the children of her first meeting with their father, but they never tired of hearing the story.

The horses on the roundabout were Ethel's favourites. She stood near them, in between rides, stroking them as they waited for the summons to gallop away! She was skilful at hoop-la, roll-a-penny and any game involving accuracy and careful judgement. People smiled at the small girl as she solemnly weighed up the situation before neatly tossing a hoop or landing a ball in the right place to win a prize. The family usually walked home with a satisfying collection of prizes, including at least one coconut, for Tom was also a good aim and had a strong right arm. Although their parents maintained the fair was a shadow of its former self, the children enjoyed it every bit as much as their elders had when they were young.

Shortly after the fair it was Harvest Supper, when the Grays invited all those who had helped with getting the harvest in to a party in the barn. Alice helped Minnie and Mrs. Gray with the food. For days they had roasted meat, boiled puddings and baked pies for the evening's feast. There was plenty of ale for the men to drink and bottles of lemonade for the children. After the meal there was music and some dancing, the farmyard ablaze with light from lanterns. Ethel loved to see the enormous harvest moon, hanging like a giant orange just above the horizon. It looked as if it must come to earth, but sailed up into the sky again as the evening wore on.

Halloween was next. Lanterns were made from scooped out swedes, and night-lights placed inside them. The children placed them round the garden, where the grinning faces leered at them as they chased round the house, playing murder in the dark and hide and seek. Although the children usually kept strictly to their side of the undivided garden, they were allowed the run of both the Grays' and the Taylors' land for this night. When they were tired out they came into Alice's kitchen, her own family and the Grays', and played apple bobbing. They peeled the apples once they had caught them, and threw the longest piece of peel over their shoulders to see what initial letter it made as it landed. This told them the first letter of their future wife's or husband's name! The women made ginger snaps and toffee apples, so the evening concluded on a sticky note. As the children got older they stayed up later and sat with their parents next to the fire, listening to ghost stories and eating chestnuts roasted on the bar of the fireplace.

There followed Christmas, which was probably the most exciting time of the year, though the children received few presents in their stockings! Father Christmas did not forget them however. They had colouring books, a jigsaw, maybe an annual, some colouring pencils, a few sweets, and in the toes of their stockings the traditional orange, a sugar pig and a penny.

The boys were in the church choir, so were busy over Christmas, walking to and fro to St. Mary's for the services. All the family went to the Christmas carol service, except for Tom Senior. He seldom attended church, maintaining that his church was the woods and the fields and nothing man built could improve on them. The children went carol-singing in the sparkling, frosty evenings, bringing neighbours to their windows and doors. Most people were glad to hear them but they knew which households to avoid. They usually came home with a store of sweets or cakes to share with their parents and the younger children.

Alice and Ethel spent hours in the scullery in the run-up to Christmas, baking mince pies and cakes and puddings. The

Christmas dinner was usually a goose, which arrived with all its feathers, so the older children helped with the messy job of plucking the bird before Alice dealt with the rest of the preparations; what the boys called, "taking out the innerds!"

The house was decorated with holly, ivy and other greenery. The children made strings of lanterns: folding, cutting and glueing with home-made flour paste. The Christmas tree was brought in on Christmas Eve and, when the children were small, their parents decorated it while they lay awake upstairs, too excited to sleep. As they got older they took part in the decorating, hanging their precious baubles on the sweet-smelling pine, and home-made decorations to supplement the grander ones. A fairy topped the tree – a tiny doll which Alice had dressed in lace and satin. Tom fixed the candles on, for it needed strong fingers to secure them safely to the branches. When the candles were lit on Christmas night the family sat near the tree and sang carols until they were hoarse.

There were a few presents under the tree. Fortunes varied, and some years the presents were grander than others. One year Ethel received a beautiful doll which she cherished and adored. It had a china face and fair curls, unlike her own straight brown chestnut tresses. Once she had a china tea-set, with little animals painted on each piece. The tea-pot had a picture of a shabby old rabbit leaning on a crutch on one side of it. "Poor Bunny Bobtail" the inscription read. Ethel did not like the picture, for it was so sad. She always kept the pot turned the other way around so she could see Joey the Clown with his wooden horse instead!

The children usually made gifts for their parents, painstakingly working away at the comb case or calendar or what ever it was in a corner of the front room over a period of weeks, during which time it was difficult to maintain secrecy! Still Tom and Alice exclaimed in delight as if they had never received such marvellous presents before! There were a lot of comings and goings around Christmas, as so many relations lived nearby. New presents usually appeared under the tree after these visits.

Ethel longed for a dolls' house. One of her best friends, Winnie Ogg, had asked for a dolls' house at the top of her letter to

Father Christmas. Ethel decided to do the same. After Christmas Winnie, who lived just along the road, came round to see Ethel. She had had a big dolls house – just what she wanted. Ethel went to see it. It was every girl's dream of a dolls' house, with a little family spread throughout the three stories.

"Father Christmas didn't bring me one," said Ethel, sadly.

"Never mind, you can share mine," Winnie assured her. But it wasn't the same at all.

Ethel felt worried as she walked home. She felt sure she had been as good as she could possibly be, but she must have done something bad, or Father Christmas would have brought her a dolls' house too. She couldn't begrudge Winnie hers, for Ethel would not begrudge her friends anything. But she was puzzled.

Winnie lived with her grandparents as she was an orphan. They were devoted and kindly guardians of their grandchild. Sadly, they lost her when she was only twelve years old. She had a hole in her heart and they knew she wouldn't live to be adult. After her death her ashes were buried on the downs, near Chanctonbury Ring, just as she had asked.

****

In September 1926 Ethel began her final school year. To her dismay, the children in the top class received the same text books as the previous year and began to repeat the work they had already done. Resources were still very limited, and the brightest pupils were certainly not stretched!

Ethel's best friend in her last years at school was Phyllis Pearce. Phyllis's mother was seriously ill in hospital, so Phyllis had to live with her cousins, the Eversheds, at Parbrook. David Evershed sat in front of the two girls. He was witty and high-spirited and his sense of humour livened up the dreariness of the lessons, although it often got him into trouble with Buzzy Wright. However, he worked hard and was one of the cleverest pupils in the school. Although frequently off school with severe headaches, he soon caught up with work, and his compositions were so entertaining he was often asked to read them aloud to the rest of the class. In spite of his apparent confidence, this was purgatory. Ethel pitied him when she saw the trembling of his hands as he stood in front of the group. It was a mystery how he could be so brimming with fun one minute and trembling with nerves the next!

Ethel and Phyllis were always visiting one another's homes. Ethel was fascinated by the Eversheds' cottage, which was packed full of books and had paintings all over the walls. She often saw Gladys there, now a young woman. Gladys had been walking out with Bert since she was fourteen and it was common knowledge that they would get married as soon as they could find a home. Ethel rarely saw her cousin since she had started work, so it was an added delight to find her at the Evershed's cottage.

Mr. and Mrs. Evershed had a sobriety about them on first acquaintance, the result of years of hard work and increasingly poor health. But they were full of humour and kindness. If Ethel met Mr. Evershed along the road he always touched his hat politely and said, "How are you my little maid?" where most men walked past with no acknowledgement whatsoever. Once he presented her with a bunch of flowers for her mother, who had recently given birth to Mollie. Although Eldred (known to his friends as Jack) was outside in all weathers, he never ceased to love the Sussex countryside. He could still find time to stop at the end of a cold spring day, to pick a bunch of violets or primroses for his beloved Maggie. She always received them with delight and almost a sense of reverence. Eldred liked a good argument and could forget his aching bones when sitting in front of the fire, having a heated discussion with his uncle or sons on some point of politics he had just been reading about in the paper. He was a Christian man, with Christian ideals, which he longed to see expressed in the world around him. He strongly disapproved of swearing, but that didn't stop him from vehemently exclaiming "Jigger nation says!" when sufficiently aroused. His wife, Susanna Margaretta, was a conscientious mother and housewife. When she was able to snatch a few minutes to herself, she shared her time between tending her precious plants and reading. She read the Bible every day, keeping it on a shelf next to her chair, and worked her way through book after book from her late father's large collection, or from the lending library. Her artistic, musical father had passed on his gifts to her, but she did not have the opportunity to use them, although she loved to sing. More often than not her "free" time would be spent darning Eldred's socks or the seat of David's trousers!

David was very much the baby of the family, having been born sixteen years after Henrietta, the eldest. By the time he started school all but Evelyn had left. By the time he left his older siblings had gone their separate ways. Henrietta, (who renamed herself Joan), was a children's nurse in Hampshire, Arthur became an estate agent in London, Bert was a local gardener and Evelyn was a dress-maker. She had learned most of her sewing skills from her mother, who had taught her daughters fine needlework when they began making their dolls' clothes. The small garments were perfectly made, with neat button-stitching, pleating and a variety of hems and seams.

Ethel grew to love her visits to this close and sometimes rowdy household, for when they were not engaged in quieter pursuits they played boisterous games and had rousing sing-songs during which everyone was urged to perform a solo. Bert and David kept the family helpless with laughter, making up parodies on popular songs of the day or seemingly endless verses full of nonsense.

Ethel's final year at school moved relentlessly forward. In January she was absent for several weeks, for her mother gave birth to a little boy, Basil, so Ethel was needed to look after the home and family. There were no more babies born after Basil, and his older sisters and brothers lavished attention on him.

Ethel was glad to get back to school and her friends. Spring passed into summer and the last few weeks of school were before them. Old traditions died hard. In the summer term it was still customary for wealthy ladies from the parish to come to the school to inspect the children who would be leaving, with a view to finding new gardeners and maids. Ethel was furious as the women passed along the row of desks, inspecting sewing, asking questions about family background, health and so forth.

"No way am I going to work for one of those old women," she declared crossly to Phyllis Pearce, now her best friend.

"Me neither. I'm going to be a nurse," Phyllis firmly replied, and she was – eventually – a sister at the London Clinic, and responsible for the health of the royal, rich and famous.

But for Ethel it was a different story. Family fortunes had slipped a long way since her Great-great-grandmother Deborah's time. Ethel's first job was as maid for a local tradesman, getting up at five o'clock to rake out the fires and light them before the family rose. The man of the house liked game for dinner and she had the job of preparing the ripe birds, which had been hanging until they were full of maggots. Ethel had to do all the jobs the lady of the house disliked. Although used to hard work, Ethel resented the endless round of drudgery. She lost weight and her fingers were permanently chapped and blistered. One Sunday in December she went home to visit her family. Tom and Alice took one look at her and declared she would not be going back that afternoon. And she didn't!

Ethel found another job with the Moyers, a Billingshurst family, and was happier than she had been in her first place. She learned a lot of new recipes from Mrs. Moyer, and wrote them in a small exercise book which was rediscovered after her death many, many years later. Still she longed to be a nurse like Phyllis, or a teacher like her grandmother.

In September, 1929 David's sister, Joan, travelled to China as nursemaid to the small daughters of Captain and Mrs. Kelly. The captain was already stationed there, and his wife and family and Joan were to join him by November. Days before Joan's departure, Gladys Helen Humphrey married William Albert Evershed at St. Mary's Church, Billingshurst. Ethel was chief bridesmaid and David the best man. He was still rather skinny – being only sixteen years old – but he was charming, good looking, highly intelligent and very good-natured, with a sense of humour which endeared him to old and young alike. He also had an enviable ability to converse with anybody on any subject, which was way beyond his years. Ethel was shy, but she knew David well, so felt totally at ease with him.

Young Ethel Taylor in the garden at Kingslea

Throughout their childhood he had regularly visited Kingslea to play football or cricket with Stan and Tom and a host of other friends. Ethel and Gladys were still very close – more like sisters than aunt and niece – so David and Ethel felt almost like cousins. Almost – but not exactly! David was very aware of how Ethel had grown up since leaving school. She was demure and pretty and he felt a new interest in her.

Mr. and Mrs. Gray Senior, who owned Kingslea Farm, lived in the big house at the end of the drive, away from the farmyard. As they grew older they increasingly relied on their son, Bert, to run the farm. They eventually decided to make good use of the spacious house and increased time at their disposal, by advertising for paying guests. Among the first people to holiday there were Mr. and Mrs. Blellock and their family. Mr. Blellock was a director of Vauxhall motor cars and caused a sensation when he first drove into the farmyard in a large and gleaming car. Wealthy they certainly were, but pretentious or aloof they were not. The Gray and Taylor children had many rides in that beautiful car – a rare experience for them. Kingslea frequently played host to children of all ages from the village and round about, and the Blellock girls joined in with games of hide and seek or cricket. The twins, Helen and Mary, were not yet old enough for school the first time they came, and were petted and fussed over by the older children. Joan Blellock, who was in her early teens, quickly became very good friends with Ethel. They played tennis together, went for walks with the younger children or just lazed in the fields talking and giggling.

Nineteen thirty proved to be a year of change for Ethel. She had been looking forward all spring and early summer to the arrival of Gladys and Bert's first baby. Helen Margaret arrived on 4th July. She was a very pretty little girl – with blonde hair and blue eyes. Ethel spent as much time as she could with Gladdy, who lived only a short walk away, often visiting with little Basil in tow. She looked forward to the day she would be married with children of her own. At that time, her life seemed to be going nowhere. This was only to be expected. She knew it was the fate of most young girls in the country to work until they met the right man, get married and raise a family of their own. But Ethel had always been a great reader and she had formed a lot of ideas in her mind. Not only that, her conversations with Joan Blellock had opened her eyes to a way of life very different from her own. Although she was a country girl and wanted to stay that way, she felt a certain yearning for the life Joan described to her. Joan passed on some of their conversations to her mother and probably this was part of the reason why, towards the end of their holiday, Mrs. Blellock asked Ethel if she would like to live with them in Cricklewood. She would be asked to help with the housework, but they would not expect her to do the kind of jobs she had been doing at the Moyers. It would be light housework and a little cooking only. Her main job would be looking after the twins and acting as a companion to Joan.

In spite of her eagerness to see the world beyond her corner of West Sussex, Ethel was not too sure to begin with. She loved her family and was easily homesick. She would not get many opportunities to visit Kingslea if she accepted the Blellock's offer. But Joan pleaded with Ethel and reminded her of the wonderful things she would be able to see and do - join the tennis club, have dancing lessons, visit the theatre and go on shopping expeditions in the West End! There would be holidays in Bournemouth – motoring down through the New Forest; boat trips on the Thames and picnics in the parks. Ethel talked it over with her parents, who persuaded her it was an opportunity not to be missed.

There followed a frantic few days as she collected her belongings together and filled her brand new tin trunk until it could take no more. It was put on the train for London the day before she was due to leave with the Blellocks, as there was insufficient room for it in the car. The Grays and Taylors gathered outside the gate to wave the party off. How Ethel's heart ached for that little group, her mother smiling and crying at the same time, and the forlorn expressions on the children's faces. Her father wheeled away from the gate, his hands thrust into his trouser pockets, and trudged away into the meadow beyond the garden as the sound of the car's engine dwindled away. The group dispersed, the children strangely silent. Ethel had been such an important part of their lives – always ready to play a game or tell a story or dry a tear.

    Letters flew to and fro between London and Sussex several times a week. If Ethel sent a letter in the morning, she knew her family would receive it that same day. Even Stan's dog received parcels in the post, addressed to "Miss Vender Taylor" and containing large and juicy bones!

Chapter Seven

Ethel spent five years with the Blellocks, during which time she did all the things Joan had promised she would – and more. She took ballroom dancing lessons and had tennis coaching, so that within a couple of years she was dancing in competitions and playing tennis for a local club in regional tournaments. Helen and Mary belonged to a ballet school, and Ethel took them to their classes and watched their rehearsals for dancing displays and ballet performances in London theatres. She learned ballet exercises from the twins and joined in their rehearsals at home. They learned the piano, too, and Ethel envied them this even more than the dancing. Each morning before breakfast they had to practice, a cause of complaint at the start of each and every day!

The Blellocks had a large and fascinating circle of friends and acquaintances. They were Christian Scientists and many of their ideas were new and intriguing to Ethel, although she seldom if ever changed her opinion on anything! She was a Sussex woman – unshakeably firm in her own convictions. Through the Blellocks she met people from the film and theatre world, the car industry, right wing members of society with royal connections, left wing thinkers and intellectuals. She was included in everything the family did. They went down the river to Kew Gardens, spent weekends in Richmond with a vegetarian family, (a great novelty then), and frequently went shopping with Joan in the best London shops, where they occasionally saw "Crawfie" in charge of Princesses Elizabeth and Margaret. The Blellocks had a close friend who had travelled the world – an independently minded lady whose traveller's tales were riveting. She adopted a python in London Zoo and on "Members Only" occasions the Blellock household went with her to visit it. Ethel declined the invitation to hold the python, but it was a good story to tell her family when she next wrote to them!

In spite of all these new and educational experiences, visits home were still the highlight of Ethel's life! She longed for her weekends off and stepped onto the train at Victoria station with a great lightness of heart. As the train sped away from the sprawl of London into the green fields her spirits soared. At first her brothers met her off the train, vying with one another to take her case. She stepped daintily onto the platform, enjoying the impression she was making on her admiring family as they took in the fashionable London clothes, the new shoes (size 2 to 3), pretty hat and gloves. The boys firmly believed no other girl in Billingshurst could compare with their sister. She made a deep impression on others, too. David Evershed met the train whenever he could. The brothers took notice and tactfully gave him the sole pleasure of meeting her! David carried Ethel's case as she told him about everything she had seen and done since her last visit.

"But whenever I am sitting in the theatre enjoying a show I think of you and my Mum and the family and wish you could be there too, and it makes me feel sad!" she confessed.

"You shouldn't. We are glad to hear all about it and want you to enjoy it," David assured her, feeling touched.

Ethel wrote letters almost every day to her family and David. Mrs. Blellock, being a perceptive and kindly woman, gave Ethel more long weekends at home and began inviting David to visit them in Cricklewood. As the years passed he came more and more often. He partnered Ethel at the ballroom dancing contests and they won prizes. He was as light on his feet as his dainty partner and they danced beautifully together.

David and Ethel were officially engaged on Ethel's twenty-first birthday – 21st February, 1934. Her parents gave a party, for which the communicating doors between their cottage and the Grays were unlocked for the one and only time! This meant there was extra room for spreading out the food and, later, dancing to gramophone records.

By the autumn of that year David's family were beset by problems. His father had a serious stroke and had to be nursed day and night. David's money had to pay the rent, as Eldred was never going to work again. Ethel and David felt despondent as they saw their dreams of a wedding and a home of their own vanishing. Ethel felt unsettled in Cricklewood. She knew David needed her support, so early in 1935 she handed in her notice. The Blellocks were very sad to lose her, especially Joan and the twins, who thought of her as another sister. Mr. Blellock offered David a job in his company, but David was needed at home. After years of close friendship and real affection, Ethel left Cricklewood and never saw the Blellocks again! The twins wrote for a time, pleading with Ethel to come back, but then their letters ceased.

Ethel worked for the Misses Beck, who had a large house at Parbrook, long since pulled down to make way for a school and new housing. They made jam and marmalade for Christ's Hospital school, which was despatched weekly by train. David's sister, Eve, had worked for them. Now she was living at Hadfold cottages, near Adversane, married and expecting a baby. In August 1936 Evelyn's son Michael was born.

The following October Eldred took a turn for the worse. Only David was living at home, but he sent word to his brothers and sisters and Ethel to come as quickly as they could. With great difficulty, Eldred used his last breaths of life to ask his family to sing one of his favourite hymns. Gathered round the old double bed, where his children had all been born, they falteringly sang "Abide with me". He listened to the very end, then peacefully left them.

After Eldred's death Maggie went to stay at Hadfold with Eve and Harry and baby Michael. David and Ethel walked over the fields to visit them at weekends. One late summer evening they met Mr. Etherington who owned Hadfold farm and cottages.

"I hear you two are wanting to git married," he said.

"Yes, when we can find a home," David replied.

"Well, I got a cottage comin' vacan' nex' to yer sister. You two can 'ave it if yer interested. 'Tis not a large rent and I knows you'll look after 'un. Be empty by end of nex' month."

Ethel and David exchanged glances and knew the answer instantly!

They were married on October 9th, 1937 and went home to their country cottage that same night.

The kitchen at Hadfold was their favourite room. The floor was flagged with huge slabs of Sussex marble, the walls built from thick local stone. Just outside the back door was an iron pump. The privy was down the garden. Baths would be once a week, (as they had been at Kingslea and Parbrook), in a large galvanised bath, which was brought into the kitchen every Friday evening. Compared with the Blellocks' labour-saving house Hadfold was primitive, but Ethel had spent more years living in a country cottage than a modern town house and this was the cottage of her dreams.

They had a pretty garden from which a small gate led into Hadfold Woods. It was an idyllic spot for the newly married couple. The summer lingered on into autumn that year and up to the end of October Ethel and David were able to wander happily through the woods and in the fields in a mellow haze of golden sunshine. They picked blackberries and crab apples for pies, jam and jelly and gathered hazel nuts to keep for Christmas. There were mushrooms in the damp meadows and plenty of rabbits to stew or roast.

When David was working Ethel was busy with housework and gardening. She took great pride in her store cupboard, bottling, salting and preserving as many fruits and vegetables as she could as they came into season. She swapped jams and jellies with Eve who took an equal pride in having a full cupboard.

Sometimes Ethel walked south over the fields into Adversane, to the shop. Each week she visited her parents, walking eastwards over the fields and up the lane past Hook's farm to Marringdean. She usually dropped in on Gladdy and her children, for Helen had a brother and sister now.

Having David's mother and sister next door was a delight. They were always welcoming and very ready to help if asked, but never intruded or offered unwanted advice, giving the newly-weds the space they needed. On Fridays, (unless it was very wet), Ethel joined Maggie and Eve on their weekly trip to Mrs. Bennett's shop at the top of Alicks Hill. They took Michael in his pram, which was piled up with groceries on the walk home. They all pushed the pram together up Andrews Hill, but still had to pause for breath when they reached the top! They bought mainly dry goods, such as canned food, flour and sugar. Meat and fish were delivered weekly.

David and Ethel had a good-sized vegetable garden. They

planted some new fruit bushes that autumn and made plans for the following spring. They wanted to grow as much of their own food as possible and made lists of seeds and plants they would need to order by late winter. As they pored over the Carter's seed catalogues they envisaged a vegetable plot which would be second to none. David constructed a chicken coop and run, in readiness for the hens which they planned to buy once winter was over.

When spring arrived Ethel was delighted to see violets, primroses and bluebells growing in profusion; drifting from the wood into the garden. Golden celandines appeared first in the shelter of a small ditch in one corner, with windflowers shining star-like above and clumps of lush lady's smock (milkmaids) a crown of delicate pink above the rest. She grew bedding and vegetable plants from seed in frames which David built in the shelter of the shed. Their vegetable plot did them credit. Tom Taylor surveyed his daughter's and son-in-law's garden with approval.

"You've done a good job there," he said, nodding his head and grinning in the slightly shy way he had.

This was praise indeed!

David was fond of his father-in-law and keen to open his mind to new ideas and experiences. The year after their wedding David and Ethel took Tom to the Aldershot Tattoo. It was a great success, apart from Tom's introduction to paper cups. David bought him a half of ale and handed it to him with a warning to not hold it too tightly. Tom was used to handling thatcher's and farmer's tools and took the cup in his grip. It crumpled in his hand and ale went everywhere!

On another occasion David persuaded Tom to accompany him and Ethel to the cinema in Horsham, something he had been trying to achieve for months.

"He won't like it you know," Alice and Ethel both warned him, but David was young and full of enthusiasm.

They travelled to Horsham by train, a rare treat for Tom. The "pictures" proved less successful than the journey. When the organist sank majestically back into the depths of the orchestra pit and the lights went down, Tom got visibly anxious. He managed to watch the Pathe News through to the end but then rose to his feet, his seat flipping shut with an emphatic bang.

"That's it," he announced. "I don' want to see any more."

He stumbled out of the oppressive, smoke-filled cinema into the light of day and took a deep breath.

"That's not it, Dad. The film's not started yet," David said, trying to persuade him back. But Tom was obstinate and was already heading for the station.

Trying to get him to eat tomatoes was as difficult. For years Tom held out against them.

"Neither fruit nor vegetable. Nasty foreign stuff."

David was more successful with this argument and got Tom to sample half of one of his own home-grown tomatoes.

"Hm. Not bad," Tom conceded. The following year he grew his own tomatoes and every year thereafter for the rest of his life.

For two years Ethel and David were blissfully happy living at Hadfold, but then Ethel miscarried her first baby, rumours of war became reality and life changed suddenly and dramatically. David volunteered to join the Royal Air Force. While waiting for his draft papers to arrive, they left Hadfold and went to live in the lodge at Beke Place with Gladys and Bert. It was large enough for them to have their own room and take their furniture and possessions. David felt happier knowing Ethel was with his brother and sister-in-law, especially now she was pregnant once again – with twins this time. Bert was in his mid-thirties and in a reserve occupation, so was not called up to fight. He and Gladdy would help Ethel if needed and her parents were only a few minutes walk away. It was a sensible arrangement, but Ethel's heart ached as they packed up and made ready to leave their cottage. Those two years were probably the happiest of Ethel's married life, for she had many hard years ahead of her.

It took months for David's call-up papers to come through, so he volunteered as an A.R.P. warden, while continuing with his job as a gardener and handyman. Everyone was trying to adjust to the many sweeping changes in their lives. Evacuees arrived in Sussex from London in their hundreds, clambering out of the packed trains at Billingshurst station, gas masks and teddy bears at hand. Gladys and Bert took four children in with their own three. By now Helen was almost ten, David seven and Janet not yet three. The older ones had mixed feelings about sharing their rooms, and beds, with strangers, but there was a war on so they cheerfully made space for the London children and got on pretty well with them for the most part.

During the summer of 1940 German air raids intensified. Standing outside at night the fighter planes were visible over the downs. When the air raid warning sounded everyone headed for shelter, the children heavy with sleep being dragged or carried from their beds.

One summer evening Ethel was sitting in the garden watching David watering the vegetables, when she felt a sudden stab of pain. Instantly she was reminded of her miscarriage and she called out in fear. An ambulance rushed Ethel to Shoreham hospital, where she lost one of the twins – a little girl.

"She would have been called Deborah," Ethel whispered sadly to the nurse.

Whilst she was in the hospital there were many air raids. Every time the eerie wail of the siren rose into the air, the nurses snatched up the babies from the nursery and put them in a large airing cupboard. The mothers stayed in their beds and prayed!

Miraculously, given the standard of obstetrics in those days, Ethel did not lose the other baby. She came home after two weeks in hospital and carried her remaining baby the full nine months.

On September 3rd 1940, exactly one year after the outbreak of war, there was a massive air raid. The entire household headed for the shelter, except for Ethel, David and Gladdy. Ethel was in labour, and the deluge of bombs fell unheeded as the indefatigable Nurse Baines, (who had arrived on her bicycle, wearing a hard hat), ably assisted by Gladys, helped Ethel to bring her baby into the world.

"It's a boy," Gladdy announced, smiling at Ethel. Nurse Baines wrapped him in a towel and handed him into Ethel's arms. Being a twin, he was tiny. But he was healthy and well.

When the raid was over and everyone emerged from the

shelter they were relieved and delighted to find Antony John Evershed safely delivered.

That September London took a battering. After dark the sky to the north glowed with massive fires raging in the capital, over fifty miles away. The evacuees wept for their parents somewhere in the middle of the flame and devastation, but thankfully they proved to be among the fortunate ones who survived the Blitz.

On one occasion the family were gathered round the table finishing their midday meal of traditional Sussex swimmers, (balls of dough boiled in water and served with syrup or sugar), when a bomb came flying over the fields towards them. The little group sat transfixed watching the path of the bomb, which went over the house and exploded at a distance. Suddenly Helen - who was usually the most scared of the bombing, being most aware of the danger - began to laugh. They turned to her as she giggled helplessly,

"Dave, you're putting salt on your swimmers instead of sugar!"

Dave laughed with the rest, for laughter came surprisingly easily at that time of great strain. When danger was over, you had to release the tension. They played the fool, sang and whistled their way through the long days of double summer time. Then came the night and the air raids.

David and Ethel looked out anxiously for the postman every morning, knowing each day was bringing David's departure nearer and praying it would not be until after Christmas.

That year the family threw themselves into Christmas preparations with an almost desperate enthusiasm, aware that an uncertain and frightening future lay before them. David and Bert wrote a nativity play for the children to act, while their wives got busy making costumes. One of the evacuees played Mary, and Antony was the infant Jesus.

All the children hung up stockings on Christmas Eve, which were filled with small things, many of which the adults had been working on during winter evenings. Eve had made soft toys and Indian head-dresses for a toy shop in Horsham before the war, so her expertise came in very useful. Everyone kept an eye open for

David & Ethel Evershed's wedding

Corporal David Evershed

feathers and when the chickens moulted not a single decent-sized feather was wasted. They were washed, painted and made into headdresses for boys and girls. Alice, Maggie, Gladys, Eve and Ethel cut down old clothes of their own to make skirts and blouses for Helen and Janet and the evacuee girls, shorts and shirts for the boys.

The older children were equally busy making things for one another and for their grown up relations. Helen knitted kettle holders and sewed comb cases and needle cases. The big children helped the younger ones to make calendars and cards for their parents and grandparents.

That was Christmas 1940. Each year it got increasingly difficult to find materials to make presents, but somehow a gift was always contrived for every member of the family. Rations were saved to put into the Christmas cake and pudding, and usual ingredients supplemented with less usual ones, such as carrots, apple and bottled fruit. The long slithers of silvery foil which the Germans dropped to interfere with the British radar were gathered from the hedgerows and used to decorate the Christmas trees.

As time passed the local woods filled with soldiers, mainly Canadians, and large houses were commandeered for the officers. One such was Beke Hall, a mansion opposite the Lodge. The locals benefited from the Canadians' generosity, especially at Christmas, when they gave big slabs of Madeira cake and "candy" to their English neighbours. The Italian P.O.W.'s who were housed in a camp on the Marringdean Road were keen to befriend their captors! They lined up alongside the fencing, keeping a look-out for mothers and children walking by, and threw them bars of chocolate from their Red Cross parcels! The Italians were very popular, especially with the children, but not purely because of their generosity. Some of them worked in local farms and gardens and proved to be industrious and good company. Mario, who worked at Beke, gave the children shoulder rides and played games with them. He became a friend to the entire family who kept up a correspondence with him for some time after his return to Italy at the end of the war.

Early in 1941 The Letter arrived. David was to go to Hereford initially, then to the north for further training. People were learning fast that one should take each day as it came and not think too long or hard about the future. David would have some home leave before his active service began, so when they allowed themselves to think beyond the moment the family tried to focus on that particular thought.

The time came when David finished his training and wrote to Ethel with the news that he had received his wings. This was both a source of pride and of increased anxiety for his family. Ethel tried to blot out her fears for her husband with hard work. She helped the war effort by working part-time at a local market garden, growing vegetables, as well as sharing the care of all the children at Beke. Of course, she had her baby to look after, which gave her great comfort. She visited Alice and Tom, who were just a short walk away, as often as she could. Stan and Tom junior were both in the army and were eventually sent abroad. Poor Alice worried incessantly about her boys, but both she and Tom stoically did their bit, fire-watching. Basil was twelve when war broke out. He longed to join the forces, like his brothers, but wanted to be in the Air Force like his Uncle Dave. His usually docile mother got cross when he complained and expressed the wish that the war might continue until he was eighteen and could fly a Spitfire!

Ethel spent hours writing letters. She wrote to David every day, and regularly to her brothers and her cousins – Dennis and Eric – who were in Africa. They were her Auntie Lot's sons and Ethel had known them since they were small. Auntie Lot and Uncle Reg were very proud of their sons, who had both gone to Midhurst Grammar School, where they had been taught science by a young H.G. Wells. They had gone on to study at Oxford, but now the war had sent them into the army.

Ethel had loved to stay with Auntie Lot as a young girl, when she and Uncle Reg lived in a bungalow deep in the woods near Coolham, although there had been one occasion when Ethel was woken from sleep by a tramp, leaning through her bedroom window, waving a billy-can and asking for a drop of water for his tea! Although Ethel had nothing whatsoever against tramps, (Alice having always given them a warm welcome and cup of tea if they dropped into Kingslea – quite a common occurrence between the wars), she had such a fright waking to find a strange and whiskery face looking down into hers that it turned her against bungalows altogether!

While David was away during the war, Ethel took an occasional short break with Auntie Lot and Uncle Reg, who had lived in and around Midhurst for some years, Reg having taken a job on the Cowdray Estate. Throughout the war they lived at Woolbeding, so Ethel took a bus to Midhurst and walked into the village from there. In spite of their concern for their sons, Reg and Lot remained cheerful and were kindly, comforting people to visit. Aunt Lot was very busy with the Women's Institute and worked hard providing help for the troops. As Antony grew older, Ethel read stories to him at bedtime, and Uncle Reg sat listening – quite entranced! Ethel enjoyed the countryside around Midhurst. Although there were fewer primroses in spring, snowdrops and lily-of-the-valley grew profusely in the sandy soil. In the summer the family often walked into the small town to picnic near the Cowdray ruins. The river was sandy and shallow enough for bathing during the summer and Antony loved paddling in the water. The seaside itself was out of bounds during the war, the beaches being covered in defences and the water full of oil.

In September 1943, while Ethel was on a visit to Woolbeding, news came on the wireless that a bomb had landed on the boys' school at Petworth, killing 28 boys and four adults. People were stunned. There had been plenty of bombs dropped in the area, but none had done damage on this scale. The following day Ethel had to catch a bus back to Billingshurst, which passed through Petworth. She never forgot the devastation and the horror.

****

David was occasionally allowed some weekend leave. Making his way across London to Victoria Station was like a surreal dream, with familiar buildings reduced to charred rubble and the underground stations full of people sheltering from possible further air raids.

On Halloween, 1941, David suffered an accident during his journey home from Barrow-in-Furness, where he was stationed. The accident probably saved his life, as it landed him in hospital for weeks, and he was unable to return to flying.

Changing trains at Crewe during the black-out, he was unaware that his train had stopped short of the station. He opened the door and fell out on to the track. The train moved on and ran over his elbow, crushing it. David was desperate to see Ethel and Antony and he did not want to end up in a hospital miles from his home, so he pulled his great coat around his smashed arm and somehow travelled back to Billingshurst. He was in agony all the time, but refused offers of help. It took him all night and much of the next day to get back to Sussex. When he arrived at Billingshurst no-one was expecting him, so he walked the long walk up to Beke. When he staggered in the family were appalled by the state he was in. Ethel and Bert went with him back to Billingshurst, to the doctor's surgery. The doctor did not attempt to look at the arm, which was so swollen Ethel had had to cut the clothes away from it. There followed a train journey to Guildford and eventually, twenty four hours after his accident, David was seen by a doctor.

David finally ended up in a services hospital at Chertsey. Ironically it was a German surgeon, who had fled from the Nazis before the war, who rescued David's arm. He rebuilt the bone around a stainless steel bolt from a Messerschmidt, which he had kept at home in his flat! Years later the sharp bolt could be felt when David flexed his arm, which was horribly fascinating to his small daughter. David's left sleeves were always darned and patched after a few weeks wear – but without the skill and quick thinking of the surgeon, he would probably have lost his arm.

It was while David was in Chertsey that Ethel had the first of two lucky escapes. She always visited Dave on the same day each week. It was a long and difficult journey, travelling by train from Billingshurst to Christ's Hospital and then to Guildford, where she had to change trains again to get to Chertsey. Ethel was always laden with Antony on one arm and bags of small gifts and cards from the family. Sometimes Auntie Ethel gave her niece pies to take for the wounded to share – blackberry, apple and even rabbit! It was not surprising that Ethel's visits were looked forward to by the entire ward! Usually a group of men met Ethel off the train. David and a mate were often in charge of a wheelchair, each one pushing their disabled friend one-handed. Antony perched on the footrest and had a ride back to the hospital.

One week Ethel decided to change her day to visit David from the usual Wednesday. That day bombs fell at Bramley and on nearby Guildford station, and many people on the train which Ethel and Antony normally caught were killed and injured.

Ethel's second lucky escape was close to home. She was pushing Antony along Hadfold Lane, returning from a visit to Maggie, Eve and Michael, when a German plane flew low across the fields. Ethel could see the pilot's face as he came towards them. She snatched Antony from the pram and leapt into a muddy ditch, which was full of nettles and brambles, holding the baby beneath her. Had he chosen to do so, the pilot could have shot her, but he held fire and flew over.

It took a long time and a lot of therapy to get David's arm fit again, but eventually he was posted back up north, this time as an instructor. Although Ethel missed him, she felt relief that he would no longer be flying. He worked well and was soon promoted to Corporal. Still full of fun and good humour, David was appointed Entertainments Officer. He was ideal for this job and arranged outings, concerts, quizzes and dances. In spite of the obvious difficulties of travelling during the war, he succeeded in organizing a trip to London to see Sir Malcolm Sargent conduct a performance of Beethoven's Emperor Concerto.

In common with the majority of men and women in the forces, David had seldom ventured more than a few miles from home. Trips to London to see Ethel were the furthest he had been until the war. Leaving his home and family at the age of twenty-six to embark on rigorous military training in Hereford and Barrow-in-Furness was a dramatic learning curve and quite a shock to the system! In spite of having to suffer the miseries of square bashing and military discipline, David enjoyed meeting men from all over the country and from all walks of life. He was desperately home-sick at times, and the migraine which had always been a problem for him began to get more severe. He collapsed on one occasion and awoke to find himself in the military hospital. But he welcomed the opportunities, scant though they were, to explore his new and alien surroundings. He loved Hereford – the beauty of the countryside and the history of the city itself. Once stationed in Lancashire, he made trips down to Blackpool and up to the Lakes. The magnificence and grandeur of the Lake District was beyond anything he had seen before. He sent postcards and letters detailing the beauty of the scenery and hospitality of the Lancastrians back to his family.

But Dave's heart was in Sussex all the while and precious trips back on leave were very few and far between. When at last the war was over, David was offered the rank of sergeant. It would have meant, initially at least, being based in Yeovil, away from Ethel and Antony. David had had enough of life in the forces and declined the offer.

Once back in Sussex life was totally different from before the war. If David had imagined things could go on as they had done, he would have been deluding himself, but he was far too intelligent to fall into that trap. He knew he had to find a home for himself and Ethel and Antony. They couldn't continue living with Bert and Gladys and their growing family.

Neither Ethel nor David were prepared for the big change that was looming on the family's horizon. It transpired there was a very good reason why they could not stay at Beke Lodge much longer and that was Bert's and Gladys's decision to emigrate to Canada. Bert's employer, Captain Corbett, was buying a farm in Ontario and wanted Bert to go out there as farm manager. The idea was tempting from the start, given the standard of living in Canada compared with Britain, which was crippled after the war and doomed to years of economic hardship, rationing and rebuilding. The lid was sealed on the offer when threats of a new war with Russia began to fill the papers. David and Ethel listened to their plans with a mixture of dismay and envy. Although neither of them really wanted to emigrate, the prospect of leaving the aftermath of war behind and seeking new horizons had a certain appeal. Primarily, though, they were desperately sad at the thought of losing that close relationship which had always been a part of their lives. If Bert and Gladdy went to live in Canada, they might never see them again. Maggie, (whom her sons now referred to as The Old Lady), did not show her feelings. She had a strong Christian faith which had sustained her during the long years of war, when her fears for David had always been there, though unexpressed. Now he was safely returned, but she was going to lose her second son.

It would take time, of course. It was not until 1948 that Bert, Gladys and their family left England for their new life in Canada, but the years between the end of the war and the time of their departure were filled with a painful uncertainty and brooding sense of impending change.

David and Ethel had to get on with their own lives, picking up the scattered pieces. Eventually David got a gardening job. It would do for a start. He also found a cottage for rent, at Adversane!

The Blacksmith's Arms in the 1950s

The malthouse cottages in the 1950s

Chapter Eight

David and Ethel walked round to Adversane to take a look at the cottage from outside. Ethel knew it was part of the old malthouse, but it proved to be the very cottage where she had heard her first wireless broadcast so many years before! It had changed somewhat in the intervening years. The current owner had had the espalier fruit trees cut down. Another floor had been added to provide bedrooms with low attics above, and red tiles replaced the old Horsham stone roof, which had been removed and sold. There were no solid walls or insulation upstairs: just a tile-hung exterior and thin asbestos panelling.

The most southerly cottage at the end of the row was now the shop, the earlier shop at Sayers having been boarded up. But a blacksmith worked in the forge, and the Blacksmith's Arms continued to provide hospitality and good local ale. The farmhouse on the north-east corner of the crossroads had become a restaurant. The pound was gradually crumbling away and had not been used for some years. Four council houses, confusingly named Malthouse Cottages, were being constructed to the west of the railway line. Other than that, the hamlet looked very much as it had done a hundred years before, with the exception of two small bungalows, beyond the new houses, and a small hut-like building sandwiched between them. This was the mission hall, built, as its name suggests, as a means of bringing Christianity to this outpost of Billingshurst parish!

Ethel and David stood on the green and looked at the cottages, while a crowd of untidy children stood and stared at them for some minutes before resuming their chasing game. Some of the cottage windows looked dirty, with grubby curtains at the windows.

"You can tell a lot about people by their curtains," Ethel said doubtfully, repeating a favourite saying of her grandmother's.

She had some misgivings, but it was a pretty cottage and it would be their own. Homes were almost impossible to come by post-war. The old prisoner-of-war camp was now housing London families who had been bombed out. Many families were living with relatives while waiting for prefabs or council houses to be built. Ethel looked across at Sayers.

"Funny to think that's where my great-great-grandmother once lived," she said rather wistfully. "And Dad's mother was born at the Blacksmith's Arms."

She turned her attention back to Number 4, Stane Street.

"Well?" David asked.

"I think we should take it before someone else does," Ethel replied. "And," she added as an after-thought, "I think Grandmother Deborah will like to know we are here!"

Ethel, David and Antony moved to Adversane in July, 1946.

All the rooms were in desperate need of a thorough spring-clean. The entire house, up and downstairs, had been painted a deep blood red. The hop-washing gulley which Ethel remembered from her visit to the cottage had been filled in, but the living room floor was covered in cheap wooden planks, which shed large and painful splinters. A neglected cooking range was on the north wall; a wooden dresser was fixed to the east wall. The tiny scullery had a large sink, and a copper which they soon discovered was not very efficient. There were three bedrooms upstairs. None of them had electricity and they were festooned with cobwebs. There was electricity downstairs, but everything had to be plugged into the light socket in the living room! There was no bathroom, just one cold water tap in the scullery and an outside w.c. The rent was 14/6d a week. They were responsible for interior decorating and the landlord for external decorating and repairs in general.

The garden was a jungle, full of sow thistles, weeds and rubbish. Antony thought it was marvellous, and amused himself exploring through the long grasses in search of grasshoppers and other insects. Once David and Ethel began to tackle the over-grown beds, so they could plant a vegetable plot, Antony was equally happy looking for "treasure" – the garden offering up a seemingly endless supply of relics. Carefully he washed each fragment of pottery or china unearthed, ever hopeful that he might find a precious piece of Roman jewellery, some Roman coins or a fossil!

A beautiful big ash tree grew just outside the back door, but it proved to be a mixed blessing, for its leaves made the tiled yard slippery and harboured a multitude of spiders which crept in through the bedroom windows on sultry summer nights.Around its trunk was a rambling rose – laden with deep pink, sweetly scented blooms, which filled the air with their perfume. This was the only flower they found. The only other asset the garden had to offer was a couple of mature gooseberry bushes! The entire garden would have to be reclaimed and replanted.

For all its disadvantages, Number 4 Stane Street was the Evershed's own home. Apart from the brief halcyon period between their marriage and the war, David and Ethel had not had a home of their own. Now they were still young and full of energy and enthusiasm and eagerly set about scrubbing, distempering, digging and planting. The cooking range cleaned up beautifully and Ethel produced some delicious meals. Such tempting smells wafted out of the window that on one occasion a line of hungry children formed outside, gazing curiously in as the family sat down to eat. Ethel stood up from the table and went straight upstairs to find some net curtains, which always hung in the big window after that!

By late summer Ethel was expecting another baby. Antony was now six years old, so there would be a large gap between the children, but he was nearly as excited as his parents by the prospect of having a sibling to play with.

After the exceptionally bitter winter of 1947, there was some warm sunshine to make up for it that following spring. The baby was due in April, but April came and went and Ethel just grew bigger and more tired with each day. By the second week of May the baby was almost three weeks late. Ethel stood at the range, wearily cooking lunch for Dave and Antony, when she felt her first labour pains. Instantly plans were put into action. David ran along to the shop to ring the nurse and the Corbetts at Beke Hall, who would let Gladys know the baby was on its way. Gladys would send someone to let Eve know, as she had offered to come and help. At this time Eve and Harry, with Maggie and Michael, were still living at Hadfold while they waited for a new council house to be built in

Billingshurst, so they were not far away. Within an hour Gladys had walked round from Beke, had a chat with Ethel and collected Antony and his luggage. Ethel was still in early labour and so she went to the door to see them off, watching the two much-loved figures as they walked away together hand in hand, Antony chattering excitedly, (his favourite toy, Pig Child, tucked under his arm), while Gladdy listened with her characteristic droll little smile on her face. A little later Eve arrived, with her over-night bag.

Ethel's labour was long and seriously difficult. Nurse Baines, who had seen hundreds of babies into the world during her many years as a midwife, could not remember such a difficult birth. All night and all next day Ethel bravely struggled to bring her baby into the world. Dr. Bousfield called, went away looking anxious, and returned later to find Ethel's condition was deteriorating. Eve cooked David some lunch, but neither of them could touch it. David went down to the end of the row to buy some tobacco at the shop. From behind the counter, Maud Sharville eyed him up and down. He looked terrible.

"You're goin' to lose her you know boy," she helpfully told him in a lugubrious tone. David went back and told Evelyn and Nurse Baines what she'd said.

"Nonsense!" the midwife tartly replied, but she was very worried. Ethel's labour was too far advanced to consider moving her to hospital for a Caesarian.

That evening Dr. Bousfield had a lengthy discussion with Nurse Baines, whose experience he respected, and they decided it would be necessary to administer a general anaesthetic and bring the baby into the world using instruments. By this time Ethel was exhausted and beyond caring what happened so long as it could all be over soon. David's anxiety increased and he waited downstairs with his sister, praying for a successful outcome.

At nine o'clock that evening the baby was born – alive, but only just. Ethel was very ill and Dr. Bousfield and Nurse Baines were too busy concentrating on helping her to give the baby attention. It was in such a pitiful state they held out little hope for its survival, so the nurse hastily wrapped it in a towel and put it under the bed out of the way. When Dr. Hopegill arrived, (the other doctor in the practice), he glanced at his colleagues and looked swiftly around the room. An empty crib stood in one corner.

"Where's the baby?" he demanded.

"Under the bed," came the terse reply. "We have to attend to mother first."

Dr. Hopegill knelt down and retrieved the small, limp bundle from beneath the bed. He laid it on the nearby table, then gently unfolded the towel from the silent infant and examined the injuries which necessary intervention had caused. Her left arm had suffered a fracture, her right arm was badly twisted and she was covered in cuts and abrasions. Most seriously, she was barely breathing.

When Ethel surfaced from the anaesthetic the first thing she saw was Dr. Hopegill alternately giving her baby the kiss of life and massaging its heart, praying, "Please may she live, God, please may she live!"

At last the baby spluttered and choked. Dr. Hopegill persevered with renewed fervour as the tiny heart began to respond. After what seemed an eternity the baby began to cry and, once begun, wailed on and on.

"Poor little one," Dr. Hopegill muttered, visibly moved as he handed the screaming baby to Nurse Baines.

"Please give her to me," Ethel whispered, and as she tenderly held the child close to her it began to calm down.

"What will you call her?" Dr. Hopegill asked.

"Deborah," Ethel faintly replied. "After my grandmother. And Evelyn, after her aunt," turning towards Eve, who sat next to the bed.

The following morning Nurse Baines swaddled Deborah Evelyn in layers of shawls, not being able to dress her because of her injuries, and handed the child to Eve, who took her by taxi to Horsham Hospital. The baby's broken arm was set and advice given on how to treat the twisted arm, which would have to be manipulated frequently for weeks in order to bring it back to its correct shape.

Later that day the children from Beke brought Antony to see

his sister, but she had to be held up at the window for them to admire, because some of the family had developed chicken-pox since Ethel first went into labour! The small boy stood on the grassy bank in front of the house and stared at the shawls and bandages. He could just see a very small face in the middle of the bundle. It was going to be quite a long time before his sister would be big enough to be really interesting. He was quite happy to go back to Beke with his cousins, even though they were all coming out in spots!

News of Ethel's difficult confinement quickly spread round the neighbourhood. The Myrams at Steep Wood had had a wedding in the family the day after Deborah's birth. They sent Ethel the flowers they had used to decorate the farmhouse. Eve filled vases and jugs with bunches and bunches of spring blooms, including golden cowslips, which filled the bedroom with a honey-sweet fragrance. From her bedroom window Ethel could look across at the Blacksmith's Arms. She thought of her great-grandmother, who had not survived to see her baby son, and of the baby son who had lived so short a life. Her own baby was recovering quickly from the ordeal of her birth and was a bouncing nine and a half pounds. Ethel felt a deep sense of gratitude and relief.

Although Deborah grew in strength, Ethel remained weak for months after the birth and even her eyesight was affected. She could not read – the words ran together. But gradually her strength returned and her vision improved once again. She worked hard, looking after her home with no labour-saving devices to help her, but she was used to this. She would have been perfectly content with her home and family, had there not been a constant cloud on the horizon as Bert and Gladys's departure for Canada grew ever closer.

Deborah was not quite two years old when her relatives left for their new life in Toronto, and so she was happily oblivious of the pain of their departure. They spent their last night in England at Adversane. Next morning they walked down the path to their waiting taxi to Deborah's chanting, "a tup of tea, a tup of tea", and the drumming of her spoon on her high chair. The taxi disappeared into the distance. Ethel closed the door on her dearest friends and took her children in her arms for comfort.

The voyage to Canada took three weeks. The weather was stormy and the seas turbulent. Bert and Gladys's son, David, became very ill with chronic sea-sickness, which escalated into appendicitis and then peritonitis. He was rushed to hospital when the ship docked and had his appendix removed in time to save his life, but he was so weak and thin he needed crutches to help him to walk afterwards. As time passed and summer sun melted the snows, life began to improve and so did David's health. Back in England the remaining members of the family closed ranks and soldiered on in the manner they had become used to during the war, filling what little leisure time they had with country walks, picnics and visiting between themselves. The September before Bert and family emigrated, Maggie received a wheel-chair for her seventieth birthday, which was promptly christened "Ada"! It helped to ease her sense of loss, as Maggie could now be pushed around the countryside to fresh fields and pastures new! Sometimes Ada was folded up, stowed on a bus, and the entire family headed off to the seaside, to explore unfamiliar territory, or to take Maggie back to revisit her childhood haunts around West Grinstead and Shipley.

News from Canada came regularly in the form of home-made newspapers, which each member of the family had contributed to. The Whitchurch Times, as it was called, was full of wide-ranging articles on all aspects of the family's new life in Canada. Bert concentrated on describing his work on the farm, Gladys told them about the stores – full of goods still unavailable in Britain. Helen was full of her new job as a telephone operator for Bell telephones, (having given up her teacher training course in Chichester to follow her family abroad). David usually wrote about the farm and the animals while Janet told of the skating parties and vast quantities of snow that first winter. The stories were illustrated with drawings and photographs, and there were always a few comic verses and cartoons which raised a smile. In return, a similar publication went back across the Atlantic to Canada from Sussex, bearing news of the family and the local neighbourhood. Parcels regularly came from Canada, too, containing comics and lollipops for the children and magazines, nylons and sweets for Ethel and David. At Christmas the parcels were bigger, and contained all kinds of treats - brightly coloured woolly hats and gloves, scented soap, slippers and books.

****

During the late 1940's and early 50's Adversane was still a peaceful corner of the world, with the exception of summer Sundays. Then there came a weekly invasion of London buses and, eventually, of motorists heading for the south coast. The rest of the week the A29 was quiet enough for the moorhens to continue crossing from Sayers to the pond behind Coe's barn on the other side of the road, with as much safety as they had in Grandmother Deborah's time! The roads to west and east saw very little traffic and children were able to play football, skipping or marbles there with few interruptions.

While peaceful in the sense that there was not a constant roar and rush of traffic, it was noisy and full of life, for the hamlet was home to a lot of children! They did not have to work as hard as their parents and grandparents had in their youth. They were sometimes given a few chores to do, but for the most part they were allowed to amuse themselves and only had to keep out of trouble! They had few toys but did not miss what they had never had. Instead they were nearly always playing outside.

The boys played conkers, chase, football and cricket either on the green or in the road. There was a system of mole runs under the green, which they turned into a complex of roads and tunnels for their battered dinky cars by carefully cutting the turf away from the roots.

The girls practiced handstands and cartwheels, (which Deborah could never do), and played singing games like "Queenie, Queenie, who's got the ball" and "In and out the dusky bluebells". When the grass grew long in the summer they hid in the long, swaying stems, chattering and making buttercup and daisy chains. Some of the older girls knew how to make rabbits out of foxtail grasses by twisting them in such a way that the stems were tucked inside while the rounded heads made the bodies, with two extra-long ones for the ears. Where the grass had been worn away nearer the cottages the girls pushed their dolls' prams, played marbles and jacks, bounced balls and skipped with long and short ropes, (often a piece of old washing line).

Crazes came and went. In the early fifties pocket money (for those lucky enough to have some) was spent on yo-yos. Some years later all the girls had to have a hula-hoop and would compete to see who could out-spin the others, sometimes keeping the hoops whirling round for an hour at a time.

Deborah's early years were secure and peaceful, with life following a distinct routine. Each morning, as soon as David and Antony had left the house, Ethel raked the ashes out from the range and began heating the oven to cook dinner later on. Deborah sat in an armchair, her feet tucked beneath her, watching her mother neatly sweeping ashes into her dustpan. Quite often the tortoiseshell cat would be swept from beneath the range looking disgruntled, dusty and rather scorched!

The ashes created a lot of fine dust, so Ethel (and sometimes Deborah) dusted each day except washday. Ethel continued to clean the house the old-fashioned way. She did not possess either a vacuum cleaner or carpet sweeper at that time, so she swept the floor with a stiff broom and the carpets with a brush, (or hung them on the line and beat them), and washed the kitchen floor on her hands and knees. She regularly polished her furniture, cleaned the silver and her brass ornaments and washed her precious best tea service, which gleamed on the dresser, and the plates which hung on the walls.

Monday was washday and Ethel was at her busiest. Dinner was invariably cold meat from the Sunday joint and mashed potatoes and peas with junket or rice pudding for "afters". The family usually ate their main meal mid-day then, so Ethel somehow managed to fit in cooking while dealing with the week's laundry.

In summer washday was not so bad. The steam from the copper billowed out of the open back door and Ethel stood the wringer on the little brick yard outside, where there was room for Deborah to turn the handle while Ethel fed the sheets and towels through the rollers. She put a blue bag in with the whites to make them whiter, she said, which did not make sense to Deborah. Shirts and dresses were dipped in a starch solution and hung crisply on the line. Sometimes Deborah was given a bowl of soapy water and told to wash her dolls' clothes, pegging them out on a piece of string slung across between the roses. Her father bought her a little clay bubble pipe, shaped at the end like a man wearing a top hat, and she blew bubbles from the top of his hat.

Deborah liked to watch one of the neighbours on washday. She was a large lady, who lived a couple of doors away. Although Ethel told Deborah to come away as it was rude to stare at people, the child could not take her eyes away, and continued to peer through the rose hedge. There was something about Mrs. Kleinberg which you could not fail to notice – she had a thick black moustache. This in itself was a great curiosity, but on Monday mornings the lady was really entertaining. She did the family wash in a galvanised iron bath just outside her back door, rubbing the clothes vigorously against a washboard and singing as she worked. Her favourite song was "I've got a lovely bunch of coconuts", which she sang very loudly over and over again, flinging her head back when she reached the chorus. Deborah soon picked up the words and mannerisms and went round the house singing at the top of her voice, "roll-a-ball a ba-all; roll-a-ball a ba-all," with the same upward inflection on the last syllable!

In wet or cold weather washday was far from fun. If the laundry was piling up it could not be postponed. The week's wash must be done, whatever the weather. The small cottage was filled with steam and Ethel was snappy as she struggled to cope with the piles of linen and clothes and prepare dinner at the same time. Wet washing had to be draped around the range to dry, so the warmly glowing coals were hidden and that made the house cold and cheerless. There was barely room to move in the tiny scullery and no space for Deborah to turn the handle of the wringer, (which frequently created a flood on the brick floor).

It was the same story in most of the houses around the hamlet, as frustrated housewives battled with obstinate coppers, temperamental wringers and baskets of wet laundry which had to be dried off somehow! From an early age Deborah was fascinated by the people around her. The blacksmith, George Carley, was a favourite of hers. He was a stocky, brown-skinned man, with strikingly white hair and teeth and clear blue eyes which twinkled out from beneath his bushy white eyebrows. George Carley's real name was Gaius, but he preferred plain George! He was always Mr. Carley to the children, for they rarely called adults by their Christian names. It would have been disrespectful. George and his tiny wife lived in one half of Griggs, opposite the forge. Every working day, rain or fine, frost or warm sunshine, he would stride over the road to the forge, shirt-sleeves rolled up and a leather apron from chest to knees. He never wore a coat, though he occasionally had a sleeveless pullover on top of his shirt. On a cold winter's Saturday the children sometimes sidled into the warmth of the forge and watched in fascination as George hammered away at his work, heating the horseshoes in the fierce flames to make them pliable, dipping them into water to cool them down with a satisfying hiss.

The shop-keeper, Frank Sharville, and his wife Maud, were good friends of the Eversheds. Frank was a thin middle-aged man, with a grey moustache and a hacking smoker's cough. He invited Deborah to call him "Uncle Frank" but as he was not a real uncle she decided to call him "Mr. Frank" instead! Maud was a thin little woman with brown-grey hair tucked into a net. She teased Deborah whenever she saw her, poking her in the tummy and telling her she was "crackers". One day the small girl lost her temper.

"You're a snug and a worm and a piece of fish," she shouted back.

Luckily Maud threw her head back and laughed. To Deborah's surprise, she did not get a serious telling-off!

The Sharvilles had an enormous and very docile German shepherd dog. Deborah loved him and had no fear of him although he was bigger than she was. The Eversheds had their own dog, Jill, a Welsh border collie. Deborah adored Jill, but still had a liking for Chum. She gave him drinks of water from a toy tea-cup and fed him dog biscuits. One day Chum was ill and Maud called Ethel and Deborah into the tiny room at the back of the shop to see him. He was stretched out along the length of the rug, eyes closed and tongue lolling out of his mouth. Deborah looked in wonder and dismay. She never saw him again as he died later that day. It was probably her earliest encounter with death and she missed her old friend. The Sharvilles quickly bought a golden labrador – Prince. He liked to recline on sacks of potatoes in the shop and shifted very reluctantly when a customer provokingly wanted to buy some! He had his own armchair in the Sharville's sitting-room. They were the first people in Adversane to own a television set and Deborah was invited to go along to watch it whenever she wanted to. She saw her first television programme just two houses away from the place where Ethel heard the wireless for the first time! Deborah sat in Frank Sharville's huge arm chair, almost lost in its depths, while Prince had his own chair. Together they enjoyed the antics of Sooty and Sweep. Antony usually joined his sister in front of the Sharville's television to watch the university boat race. The indistinct grey images of the two boats moving down river like black stick insects would not impress today, but it was the height of technology then.

Further along the row, beyond the Sharvilles, lived the Aherns. Their youngest daughter, Rosemary, was the only one living at home when Deborah was small. The big girl made a deep impression on the little one. She once made Deborah some ketchup sandwiches for a snack – what a delicacy! There were framed certificates around the Ahern's walls, which one of their daughters had received for her achievements as a manicurist and hair-dresser. Mrs. Ahern was the person to ask if you wanted to know what was going on in the hamlet. As she worked in the shop, not much passed her by, but she was a very kind and sympathetic soul and her interest in the life of the hamlet was sincere and concerned.

The Stillwells lived on the other side of the Eversheds – father, mother, six children, ages ranging from tot to teenage, and Floss, the alsation dog. The youngest girl, Thelma, was two years older than Deborah. Sometimes they played together and Thelma taught Deborah how to play with two balls at once, skipping and ball game rhymes and the best way to make mud pies!

In a tiny cottage at the end of the row lived Nathaniel and Abigail Tullett. Everyone respected the Tulletts – a survival from the Victorian era who retained something of the period, in spite of having come through two world wars. Weather permitting they sat side by side, framed by the cottage porch, like one of the sentimental rural idylls popular with Victorian artists. Nathaniel was quite tall, though his shoulders were bent with age. He always wore a checked cap on his snow-white hair, a jacket, white collarless shirt and black boots, and he had a large silver pocket watch in his waistcoat. It was always accurate, so the children playing on the green knew who to ask when they suspected bed-time was approaching, (and they approached him with respect and asked very politely!) Nathaniel smoked a curved pipe, and the pleasant, aromatic smell of it hung in the air on a summer's evening. Abigail wore a white lace-trimmed cap on her thin grey hair and a white apron over a neat, long dress. While Nathaniel pottered in his tiny garden, Abigail cleaned every inch of their home with exemplary thoroughness, right down to scrubbing the step every week. They had no children themselves, but were fond of them, and children were drawn to them. So long as they had one another, they were content with their frugal, yet peaceful existence. When Nathaniel died the neighbours felt sure Abigail could not survive long without him. For a few weeks she sat alone in the porch – a forlorn, frail little figure. It was just a matter of weeks before she joined her husband.

Just round the corner from the Tulletts lived Mr. and Mrs. Bond. Mr. Bond also smoked a curved pipe, but it gave out clouds of smoke and smelled like a bonfire. It was surprising he did not set fire to his woolly hat, which he insisted on wearing unless there was a really sweltering heatwave. On those rare occasions when he removed it, to see his bald head without its usual covering was almost shocking. If he had removed his trousers it would have been nearly as surprising! Mr. Bond felt strongly about a lot of things. Life was full of aggravations. He leaned across the shop counter, discussing politics with Mr. Sharville, the white pom-poms on his blue woolly hat swinging violently from side to side as he jabbed the air with the end of his pipe. He tended to splash as his temper rose and the counter sometimes needed a quick wipe down with a damp cloth after he had left the shop. The Bonds lost their only son in the war, which perhaps explained the anger which sometimes spilled over, although the anger was rarely directed at individuals. The Bonds kept themselves pretty much to themselves, but were friendly and kindly people.

Miss Dryden lived at Juppsland, which was an imposing house, although not as old as the surrounding houses. Miss Dryden was an Irish woman whom, it was said, had turned to farming as a cure for a broken heart. She was reputed to have once shown great skill as an ice-skater, but turned her back on her earlier life, finding solace in the company of animals. As the years went by she had as little to do with other people as possible and gave the impression she regarded most of them as fools. It was not always like this, however. When Deborah was about three years old, Miss Dryden gave a party for all the children in Adversane. She threw her house open and the children arrived in large numbers, dressed in their best and full of excitement. None of them had ever been inside Juppsland and parties were a very rare treat. Bearing in mind a lot of foods were still rationed Miss Dryden did them proud, with plates piled with sandwiches and cakes. She organized games and even gave a gift to each child at the end of the afternoon. Deborah's present was a clockwork police car, which drove round and round in circles, until she overwound it and the spring uncoiled!

Although Miss Dryden was an attractive woman, she took no trouble with her appearance. Her curly hair was often full of straw and her weather-beaten face seemed to have forgotten how to smile. Week in and week out she wore the same clothes – a pair of corded trousers, a shirt and a man's jacket. All were full of holes and smelt of the farmyard.

Miss Dryden owned a car which was as distinctive as its owner and nearly as notorious in Billingshurst as it was in Adversane. It was a dilapidated, cream sports car, encrusted with mud and manure and held together by string and faith. There was a hood on it originally, but eventually this failed to work, so the car was open to the weather. Because the doors were held on with binder twine Miss Dryden had to climb over them to get in and out. The car's arrival was ususally heralded by loud bangs and clankings, and sometimes bits dropped off, but it kept going for a number of years. Eventually it gave up altogether, and Miss Dryden bought a navy-blue van instead, which worked rather better and was not at all entertaining.

Juppsland was a mixed farm and Miss Dryden attempted to look after it more or less on her own, her farm hands rarely staying for more than a few weeks. She kept a small herd of cows, pigs and poultry. She also had two horses. One was a beautiful piebald pony which was rumoured to have come from a circus. Miss Dryden often tethered it on the green in front of Juppsland, and when the West Chiltington band played outside the inn on summer evenings, which it did throughout the early fifties, the pony reared onto its hind legs and, to the delight of the neighbourhood, waltzed round and round to the music!

One of Miss Dryden's favourite animals was a pet pig which lived in the house with her and the dogs and cats. It often came shopping with her, trotting behind her on a piece of string. When it was a piglet Miss Dryden sat on the shop chair with it on her lap, but as it grew too big for that it sat on the floor instead. Sometimes Miss Dryden took a lunch break in the shop, munching a piece of cheese freshly cut and washing it down with undiluted blackcurrant juice. All the while she complained to Mr. Sharville and Mrs. Ahern about something – usually the unreasonable behaviour of her cowman or her paying guests! In fact, they often had considerably more to complain about than she did!

During the summer people arrived at Juppsland by car, taxi or bus. Because the bus stop was opposite their home, the Eversheds often noticed little groups of people disembarking carrying large suitcases, and looking hopefully around for their holiday hotel. The same people could be seen escaping on the bus back home within a day or two! A common complaint was that breakfast had not arrived, and on seeking out their hostess she was discovered fast asleep on the kitchen floor with her beloved dogs!

Miss Dryden clearly did not spoil her guests. Ethel was amused to witness her in the shop one morning, counting up her guests on her fingers and then buying the same number of sausages for their evening meal! On another occasion Deborah was trying to decide how to spend her few pennies when Miss Dryden came into the shop carelessly carrying a saucepan, with a liquid jelly slopping about in it.

"Could you put this in your fridge Mr. Sharville? It's too hot for it to set in my kitchen and I want it for dinner tonight."

He did, but whether it set is questionable!

Because the farm was not a profit-making concern, by any stretch of the imagination, Miss Dryden could not keep her employees. She quite simply had no money to pay them. After a few weeks a confrontation would occur and invariably ended with the cowman returning to his tied cottage to discover all his furniture in the middle of the road! If the residents noticed a long line of cars building up they knew the chances were either Miss Dryden had evicted her latest employee or her animals had got out of the fields. Because she could not afford to maintain her fences, cattle and horses frequently escaped. Worst of all, the bull got out with frightening regularity. Having been kept shut in a pen for weeks on end it would be fumingly angry. On one terrible occasion it gored a young cowman and he was seriously injured. One afternoon Deborah opened the Evershed's back door and found a huge black bull standing on the garden path, snorting and stamping. She slammed the door and shouted for her mother, who did not believe her at first. But the bull had pushed its way round the back of the cottages and trampled across the fences between the two end gardens into the Evershed's. In spite of her fear, Deborah felt compassion for the animal as it was led roughly back over the road to its dismal, dark pen. It was only a matter of time before it broke out again.

For country children growing up at that time, the surrounding countryside was a giant playground full of possibilities. Mothers were glad to get the children from under their feet. They did not worry about their welfare when they were out in the fields and woods, for the older children could be relied on to look after the younger ones, who quickly learned the safest places to cross the ditches and streams, which plants you could chew, which berries were safe to eat, and which fields had to be checked carefully for bulls before entering. You never ever entered a field without carefully scanning it from one end to the other to ensure it was bull-free. Farmers often kept their bulls confined in small spaces for long periods at that time and then the animals would be raging once let out into the fields.

Antony and Deborah had several frightening encounters with bulls. On one of these occasions they had checked the field out before crawling under the fence, but could not see any animals. However, the field was long and sloping and so they moved with caution. As they reached the top of the incline they heard an angry bellow and a massive bull was staring at them from the far side of the field. It lowered its head, bellowed again and began to run towards them, its hooves thudding in the soft grass. Antony valiantly called to it to attract its attention and ran in one direction, giving Deborah's short legs time to race for the nearer fence. She touched the wire as she dodged beneath it, receiving an electric shock which felt like the nip of a giant lobster! But that was preferable to being tossed by the bull. On tenter-hooks, crying with fear and dread, she waited in a copse next to the field for her brother, terrified he had not escaped in time. After what felt like an eternity of waiting he appeared in between the hazel trees, his freckled face a shade paler but still grinning!

As Deborah grew up she often joined the other children on expeditions into the countryside. They played games of Robin Hood in the woods, with everyone wanting to be a goody, firing bracken stem arrows from home-made bows at the imaginary baddies! Making camps was always popular. There were a number of these in different locations, fiercely defended by which ever group of children had made them! Imaginary horses galloped over the fields to these secret hide-outs, jumping ditches and cantering tirelessly round the edges of the fields, (for the children knew better than to gallop through crops or hay). If they came up against electric fencing they listened carefully for the ticking which told them if it was switched on, and wriggled under very carefully if it was! The sharp retort of guns sent them running swiftly in the opposite direction and they knew the copses which were used for raising pheasants so tended to avoid them. Some farmers were less friendly than others and extra vigilance was needed if venturing on to their land. The children would never attempt to interfere with machinery or farm vehicles. None of them possessed a watch, but they instinctively knew when it was dinner or tea-time, (their inside clocks were totally reliable), and they hurried home with no injuries worse than the occasional deep scratch, quickly bound up with someone's grubby hanky! Mosquito bites could be a problem, especially if the children had been to the woods near Lee Place, which were home to especially vicious ones.

Often Antony and Deborah walked alone, sometimes building their own camps, damming streams, playing complicated imaginery games which involved all kinds of adventures. On other occasions they would simply explore the countryside, catching freshwater shrimps, (and releasing them again), waiting silently for a rare glimpse of the otter which lived in Brockhurst Brook, or watching hares boxing in Long Meadow. They went in search of orchids in the woods, Antony having discovered some rare bee and butterfly orchids. They looked in wonder, but never picked them. They did pick wild strawberries, which grew in profusion in certain favoured spots. In spring there was a favourite bank which had three differently coloured varieties of violets growing on it. The scent of them, especially the white ones, was deliciously sweet and pure, and they picked a small bunch to take home for their mother. Having this freedom to roam and play gave them a respect for wild life and an abiding love of the countryside which fed their imaginations and their souls.

****

It was possible to survive without venturing out of Adversane. Milk was delivered daily by Mrs. Gosling from St.

Andrew's Farm – a round-faced lady with neat grey plaits wound round her head. Meat came from a Billingshurst butcher and was either delivered by van on Saturday mornings or sent down as a parcel on the bus during the week. A fresh fish man came once a week, which usually meant sprats for Friday night tea, and a mobile fish and chip shop on a Saturday evening. Ethel did a certain amount of shopping in Billingshurst, still faithful to Mrs. Bennett's shop at Alick's Hill for some of her groceries, while clothes and shoes were bought at Bernard Baker's and Trevelyan's respectively. The clothes she purchased were usually underwear and menswear, as Ethel either made her own and Deborah's dresses and skirts, or asked Eve to make them for her. Jumpers, cardigans and socks she always knitted. Occasionally she ordered something from a catalogue – gabardine macintoshes for the children to wear to school, or grey trousers and skirts again for school wear. The bulk of the food shopping was done at Frank Sharville's shop, at the end of the row of cottages.

There was still the "secret" cellar under Mr. Sharville's shop. The Allens' escapades of the previous century had been embellished as years passed by. It was now said that the cellar had an entrance to a secret smugglers' tunnel, leading under the road into the inn opposite! David Evershed and Frank Sharville decided to investigate and went down with a couple of powerful torches to see what they could find. The cellar was still there just as it had been left, but there was no evidence of a secret tunnel, to Antony's great disappointment.

The shop was the hub of the community. Nowadays it would have come in for plenty of criticism. Nobody complained about Prince, the Sharville's elderly dog, who liked to sleep on the sacks of vegetables. People were not fussed about trivial things like the stationery being kept next to the bacon and cheese. If there were spots of grease on your postcard you simply wrote around them or put up with your pen sliding a bit!

It was not easy stocking such a small shop and Frank Sharville took a pride in trying to supply as many of the necessities of life as he could in the small space available. Things had to be put close together to fit them all in. If you were asked to help yourself to something it was quite a challenge. A stranger might well spend several minutes scanning the shelves for a light bulb, for instance. He might try looking in the corner where the candles and matches were kept, or try the household cleaning section. It would be with a sense of triumph that he finally discovered the bulbs, sandwiched between the tinned meat and shampoo.

As well as running the Post Office and providing basic groceries and household needs, Frank Sharville liked surprising his customers with unexpected extras which he squeezed into odd corners. Haberdashery was stowed in the bottom of the smoking cabinet, birthday cards were secreted in a corner by the soup, stockings and jiffy hoods were under the counter. New and exciting lines were placed on the counter, in prime position. Exotic fruits like lychees and blood oranges, new brands of anything from soap powder to cereal, chocolate to razor blades, were given pride of place on the top of the counter.

Deborah knew she was growing up when she was first entrusted with the job of going "down to the shop". It was not worth hanging about outside, gazing into the window at rows of tempting sweets or goodies, because they didn't exist in this village shop window! The window display usually consisted of some rather muddy scales and a sack of potatoes and a few fading Post Office notices, except at Christmas when an effort was made to brighten it up a bit!

Being too small to reach the door knob, Deborah had to suffer the embarrassment of knocking the big black door with her small knuckles until help came from within. A distant voice would declare, "I bet that's little Debby Evershed, let her in would you Fred, (or George or Bert)." A giant person would hold open the door for her to go in, clutching her handful of coins and mentally going through the short list of items she had to buy! What a relief when she found she had grown tall enough to open the door herself, making the Oxo sign, which was suspended from the letter-box, swing to and fro with a clanking noise which acted as a shop bell in quieter moments and summoned help from the depths of the scullery behind the shop! More often than not she went shopping in the late afternoon when the shop was at its busiest.

Most of the customers around five o'clock were labourers coming in for tobacco and cigarette papers before going home to their cooked dinners. There were sometimes other children, spending their pocket money or doing shopping for their mothers. The lucky ones with pennies to spend gathered round the small selection of sweets, wishing they had enough for a quarter of toffees or big bar of chocolate and making do, after agonising moments of indecision, with a penny toffee strip or bar of "Five Boys" chocolate. Mr. Sharville did not mind how long they took to decide. Neither did his assistant, the Evershed's next door neighbour, May Aherne. She smiled and nodded at the children. Nobody was pressurised. There was all the time in the world! The adults continued with their laughter and talking and the continuous murmur of voices wrapped itself about the younger customers like a comfortable shawl. Some of the gossip filtered into Deborah's ears and registered in her mind, in between thoughts of what to buy. The shop was a hot bed of gossip. Local people knew that what ever happened in the community the shop would hear of it first! If someone was taken ill, the details could be ascertained in the shop. If new people moved in the size of family, husband's occupation and where they had come from were quickly discovered by some strange magic and the information spread quickly from the shop outwards! There was a positive side to the gossip, for newcomers were made to feel welcome and anyone going through some trauma or tragedy would receive many kindnesses from the other members of the close little community.

As the nights drew in during September and October it was dazzling and noisy coming into the shop after the soft darkness outside. In autumn there was one big attraction for the Adversane children, for the tall glass cabinet to the left of the door, which usually contained sponge cakes and biscuits, underwent a transformation. Instead of ginger slab cake and Madeira cake there were boxes of fireworks! Ethel and David's wedding anniversary was in October, so Antony and Deborah saved up their pocket money to buy fireworks for a special celebration! There were no rules about children buying fireworks then and the two of them spent many happy minutes in front of the cabinet, looking at their money and trying to decide what to buy. The fireworks were usually chosen for their names – Mount Vesuvius, Rain of Stars, Snowstorm, Roman Candle and Golden Rain. They usually got at least one Catherine Wheel and a rocket to finish the proceedings off nicely! The fireworks were stored under Antony's bed in a wooden box (which he had made in a carpentry class). Every day the children looked over their precious store and added another one or two if they could afford it. Antony could sometimes earn some extra pennies by doing small gardening jobs, which helped to swell the funds.

    Because Frank Sharville was a good friend of David's, (they went to Brighton together to support the Seagulls!), he kept a special eye out for Deborah. If there were no other children in the shop he would ask her to try a new sweet, or an apple from a crate just delivered "to see what they're like"! Her two ounces of Tom Thumb drops or Dolly Mixture was often nearer four ounces and if there were a few odd sweets left in a jar he would ask her if she would like them – what a question! She went home clutching a bag half full of sherbet lemons or aniseed balls feeling very pleased with herself.

Frank Sharville & David Evershed dressed for a Victorian charity cricket match

Fancy dress parade in the early 1950s

Great grandparents Humphrey

Chapter Nine

Ethel felt a deep concern for her children's souls and taught them to pray as soon as they could string a sentence together. There being no church in Adversane and no transport to get them to Billingshurst at the right time for a service, Ethel was pleased when a notice appeared in the shop announcing that regular services and a Sunday school would soon recommence in the Mission Hall, after a lapse of several years.

The Mission Hall was a dull-looking building, built from the cheapest materials and disparagingly referred to by the children as "the dog kennel". Although intended to bring religion into the lives of this rather neglected corner of Billingshurst parish, the original purpose was gradually eclipsed by the profane uses the locals found for it. Not that there is anything wrong with people enjoying themselves, and the Mission Hall provided a venue for much needed hilarity in the somewhat austere period after the war. For a few years in the early fifties, though, there was a weekly service in the hall, preceded by Sunday school. The congregations were small but committed. The Rev. Langton was popular, and so was his daughter, Jane, who taught the Sunday school. After they moved to another parish attendance began to decline. The new vicar was over-heard to remark that there were more heathens in Adversane than darkest Africa, which outraged a lot of people and amused some of the more cynical ones.

Deborah looked forward to Sunday school. She liked the gentle approach of the youthful teacher, and enjoyed the hymns. Most importantly, she wanted to add to her collection of pictures of Bible stories which were given out, one each week, to be stuck into a small album provided for every pupil. If you missed a week you didn't get your sticker, so were left with an untidy gap in the album.

One wild and stormy morning Deborah found she was the only child at the hall. There was no Sunday school because it was school holidays and a communion service was being held instead. The vicar, his daughter and the harmonium player were the only people present, apart from Deborah. After a few more minutes of peering hopefully out of the streaming wet windows the Rev. Langton sighed and said glumly, "Well, I suppose three are gathered together...." This reminded Deborah of a poem which her father sometimes read to her about Eddi, priest of St. Wilfrid, who had conducted a service for an ox, ass and bullock. It was such a wild and stormy morning she half-expected a "wet, yoke-weary bullock" to push its way in through the door. No-one suggested Deborah might like to go home and she felt rather flattered to be included in the small but select congregation. But the service seemed interminable and she could not follow it. This combined with the misery of trying to sing unknown hymns to the highly-pitched harmonium accompaniment, whilst standing next to the Vicar himself, quite put Deborah off Sunday school. She would not go unless she could be sure someone else would be there too, and nearly all the other children had either dropped away or came very occasionally. She never succeeded in filling her album with stickers and had to content herself with admiring the few she had!

There was still a healthy congregation for the main church festivals. The children were encouraged to help with the Harvest Festival by collecting fruit, flowers and vegetables from the neighbourhood. Under the watchful eye of Mrs. Farquharson from Adversane House and Mrs. Izard from Glendale they were then permitted to help with the decorating, carefully lining up rows of carrots, onions, apples and pears along the narrow window sills.

Easter provided another opportunity to brighten up the sober building, transforming it with bunches of spring flowers. The Adversane children went out across the fields and into the woods to pick as many different kinds of flowers as they could. There was an air of competition about it, with children trying to out-do one another in picking the biggest and largest number of bunches. Wild flowers were plentiful then, and there were always plenty left growing after the children had taken their share. They would not pick all the flowers from one clump, and rare flowers like orchids were left alone. Wild daffodils, primroses and bluebells were so prolific that older children used to sell them at the roadside to weekend motorists, having spent the morning picking and then stringing their bunches on to long sticks to carry them home. It was also the custom to bring bunches of primroses to school each spring, which were carefully packed in boxes and sent by train up to London, for school children there.

It was not only religious festivals which transformed the hall. It happened to an extent each week. For six days out of seven it bore no resemblance to a place of worship. The harmonium and altar were draped with cloths, the candlesticks and wooden cross stowed away and a gramophone and box of records took pride of place on a table in front of the altar. Music regularly blared out of the hall and carried through the night air as far as the Blacksmith's Arms. There was Scottish dance music on Tuesdays; ballet music on Fridays, followed by pop music as the ballerinas gave way to the youth club. Live music was even louder, provided by a highly popular skiffle group.

The driving force behind many of the activities in the hall was Lola Baxter, a tremendously vibrant and enthusiastic ex-ballerina who taught the ballet lessons. She also organised the Scottish dancing, social and youth clubs, carol-singing and any number of events from beetle and whist drives to parties and socials. She regularly arranged variety shows and dancing displays, in aid of charity. These were held at the Women's Hall in Billingshurst eventually, but there was an early attempt at presenting an entertainment in the Mission Hall, using the talents of the social club.

The ladies cloakroom at the rear of the hall, which was the size of a larder, served as a dressing-room for both sexes, as the gentlemen's facilities were outside the hall and consisted of a w.c.only. This shared arrangement meant there was a certain amount of rather anxious waiting for the performers whilst which ever sex was inside the cloakroom got changed as fast as they could so they could make room for the others! The audience chatted happily throughout the inevitable delays.

Towards the end of the show there was a colourful pageant entitled "Marriage Through the Ages". First on was Jim, a local character who had come to live in the country after being bombed out of London. As a caveman he had to drag his unfortunate partner in by her long hair with one hand, while waving a club in the other hand. Earlier he had asked what cavemen wore under their fur skins, receiving the obvious answer – nothing. The old fur coat, which Jim had slung on to look as much like a dead animal as possible, slipped off when he was half way across the floor! Being such a small building, chairs had been packed tightly into rows with the first row almost on the "stage". Some of the audience seated in the front received a nasty shock when Jim's fur fell off. This was probably one reason why it was decided not to use the Mission Hall for this kind of entertainment again!

When Deborah was four years old Ethel took her to see Lola Baxter, who lived at Old House with her partner Anona Frame. They ran an antiques business and the restaurant and at that time lived on the premises, which were large and rambling. The reason for the visit was to ask if Deborah could join the ballet class. Ethel still had vivid memories of Helen and Mary Blellock's dancing classes and Deborah's enthusiastic dancing to the wireless encouraged her to find out if her daughter was old enough to start learning.

Lola Baxter was on her knees weeding a flower bed, but still managing to look quite glamorous, as she always did. She adored children, and beamed a welcome as Ethel and Deborah came up to her. They were invited inside, where Deborah gazed around at the beautiful antiques, especially three enormous coloured glass balls suspended from low oak beams. After a few formalities it was agreed Deborah should come to watch the next rehearsal. Normally the girls danced in the hall, but this was an extra practice so would be in Old House itself, the hall being used for a different event. Antony got the job of taking Deborah to watch and sat rather awkwardly, with Deborah on his lap, while the girls (who looked enormous to the four year old) went through their dances for The Toy Shop. Deborah was captivated. Once the other children had performed their show and were back to normal lessons, Deborah joined them.

There was no barre or mirrors in the hall, just two lines of chairs down either side of the room. The bigger girls held on to the tops of the chair backs, the small ones the sides of the seats and the inbetweens on to various parts of the uprights in the chair backs. The girls' ages ranged from about fifteen to four. They all wore a uniform. Deborah's granny and Auntie Flip quickly made her the regulation sleeveless black tunic, with pale blue ribbon trimming round the neck and arms. She took a trip into Horsham with her mother, where they bought a beautiful pair of red ballet shoes, (which were acceptable, although it turned out afterwards she should have had black!), and some black knickers. Ethel made a pale blue hair band from ribbon and elastic, (which slipped off Deborah's short, fine hair). Wearing a cardigan over her uniform, Deborah proudly walked round to the Mission Hall, ballet shoes in one hand, the other holding tightly to Ethel.

So Deborah began what was to be over a decade of dancing classes and ballet shows. Most of these were held in Billingshurst, but the girls danced for village fetes in Billingshurst and Amberley. They sometimes joined the social and youth clubs in putting on pantomimes, and although these invariably ran well behind schedule, on one occasion being performed in mid-summer, they were hugely popular in the village. The dancing class had a good reputation, and girls joined from Pulborough and Billingshurst. After dancing lessons in the tiny Mission Hall, the Women's Hall seemed palatial! Deborah looked around her at the vast space with awe. There was a real stage too and big sepia pictures hanging round the walls of stern looking ladies in plain clothes who, Ethel told her, were the very kind Miss Becks, who had had the hall built for people to enjoy. They had also been responsible for providing the adjacent Mother's Garden.

1953 was coronation year and the country was caught up in a frenzy of preparation. Every community, however small, wanted to celebrate. Adversane being part of Billingshurst parish, the children were all invited to a party in the village, where they would each receive a coronation mug. The village was having a procession of floats, but Adversane was very much a separate part of the parish, so it was decided it would have its own procession and travel in

Susanna Evershed in her seventies in "Ada"

suitably regal fashion along the A29 to Billingshurst. The Social and Youth Clubs and ballet class were all involved, and for weeks every spare moment was taken up with making paper flowers and red, white and blue costumes and decorations.

Coronation Day dawned cold and wet, but the nation made a determined effort to ignore the weather. Deborah was on a float representing the seaside. She would have preferred to be the Queen, wearing a red velvet cloak and jewel-studded crown, and holding an orb in one hand, but a big girl called Sylvia White was given that honour. Deborah wore a red, white and blue swimsuit, trimmed with frills, and matching sun-bonnet. Because it was so cold, she also wore two woolly jumpers underneath! She proudly made her way across the road, clutching her seaside bucket and spade, to where the floats were assembling. Someone hoisted her onto the trailer, with instructions to play in the sand and not get near the edge, especially once they got moving. She looked around for the sand and found a pile of it under a large umbrella. Sitting in the sand, looking rather lonely and forlorn, she spotted another little girl from the ballet class. Together they tried to make castles in the dry sand as the tractor dragged their lurching trailer up the road to Billingshurst and all round the council estates. They were not alone of course. A young woman in a bikini sheltered from the intermittent rain under their umbrella, her teeth chattering with cold. Deborah pointed out her own warm jumpers, suggesting it might have been a good idea to wear something over the bikini, which made the young woman laugh. When the rain eased she left the shelter of the umbrella and tossed a beach ball to and fro to a man. Deborah did not take a lot of notice of the others on the float, having to concentrate on the sand castles and not falling over! It seemed a long way to Billingshurst, but they were there at last. She felt important as she waved at school friends standing at their gates to watch the procession go by. To her surprise, Deborah's mother was standing at the gate in Frenches Mead with her granny and Aunt Flip, having got ahead of the procession by catching a bus. The float finally came to a halt in fields on the edge of the village, where there were crowds of people enjoying a party. Deborah's family mysteriously appeared to greet her and she was taken to join the other children who were eating buns and drinking orange squash. Shortly afterwards came the presentation of the mugs, and Deborah and Antony each received one of these to stand on the dresser with the precious china.

In the late fifties Mrs. Baxter and Miss Frame moved to Clevelands in Upper Station Road, Billingshurst, leaving Old House with a resident manager. Each summer the ballet class was invited to a party and Clevelands was a perfect place to hold them. It was a magnificent house with a large and rambling garden. There were mysterious pathways leading through the shrubbery, beds of fragrant roses, and a walled garden at the back containing glass houses and large beds of vegetables and soft fruit. A semi-circular lawn fronted the house. This was raised above a large paddock, where retired seaside donkeys and mining ponies spent their last years in great contentment.

The parties were exceptional! There were games on the lawn, treasure hunts around the garden and once, an inspired idea of Mrs. Baxter's, a contest to see who could pick the most blackberries, the resulting baskets and punnets of fruit going to her cook for jelly and jam-making. Tea was on the lawn, with long tables laden with all kinds of delicacies. The mothers were not neglected. In return for their hard work, making costumes and helping in various ways, they were given caviar and other luxuries which rarely came their way.

****

During the early fifties few people had a television set, so when monthly film nights began at the Mission Hall they were highly popular. Because they were on Fridays, the dancing class had to come to a swift conclusion. The girls found it difficult to concentrate once Ernie Ayres arrived, bringing the projector, screen and an assortment of lights. A few lucky ones stayed behind to watch the films, while the others – usually the youngest or those who had to catch buses back home – reluctantly put on their outdoor shoes and coats and left the hall, now buzzing with excitement. The

Youth Club was cancelled on Film Nights, but the local youth were happy to lounge about in the back of the hall with their bottles of Pepsi and Coke, crisps and cigarettes, emitting the occasional cat-call or wolf-whistle if the films demanded it.

Deborah was allowed to stay for some of the evening's entertainment, Antony coming round to join her. Their parents seldom came. They preferred to listen to the wireless or peacefully read their books or local paper. This was understandable as the atmosphere in the hall became increasingly fetid and smoky as the evening wore on. The combined effects of a room full of cigarette smoke and closely packed humanity, (not a few of whom had come along straight from their work in the farmyard), was not for the faint-hearted. In spite of the heat and stuffiness, there was a keen draught through the windows, and Deborah's feet grew cold as ice. Her eyes stung with the smoke and tiredness, but nothing would make her confess to feeling tired. If asked she emphatically denied it. Cartoons were shown first, so young members of the audience could be led off halfway through the evening without feeling too cheated. Deborah's favourite cartoon characters were Mickey and Minnie Mouse and Goofy, but she shut her eyes when Popeye's grimacing features appeared on the screen. She hated his bulging eyes and ugly face! Ethel usually came to fetch Deborah home around 8.30. Backward glances at the main feature as she was buttoned up and led away usually revealed a lot of men in belted macs and pork pie hats, who spoke in American accents and fired guns at one another, so Deborah was quite happy to leave the hall. She enjoyed the short walk home through the quiet darkness, the noise of the film receding behind her. She was allowed to stay later occasionally, if the film merited a late night. She was able to watch "Great Expectations" and "The Count of Monte Cristo" because they were "classics", and if there was a Laurel and Hardy or Charlie Chaplin double bill she was also allowed to stay on! It was bliss to lean back on a hall chair, oblivious of the hardness of the seat, munching Smith's crisps and getting ever more deeply drawn into the adventures of Pip, or giggling at Laurel and Hardy's escapades.

The family visited the cinema fairly regularly. There were

two cinemas in Horsham – the Ritz and the Odeon. It was a real treat to go to the cinema, or "pictures". There was always an A and a B film then. Sometimes the films were equally good, or bad! With the Pathe Newsreel, forthcoming films and advertisements cinema-goers had their money's worth, especially if they had the time and stamina to sit through the entire programme twice. There were a few occasions, as Deborah grew older, when she went to the cinema with her brother and they watched the whole programme through once, then stayed to watch just the main feature again. It was weird going into the dark cinema on a sunny afternoon and later emerging from the bright foyer into the dark evening streets. Invariably, both children developed sick headaches after so many hours with their eyes glued to the screen, and felt distinctly ill as the double-decker bus jerked them the long way home to Adversane.

****

Without the Mission Hall, undoubtedly life in Adversane would have had few entertainments or diversions. There was one major event, however, which the children looked forward to with as much eagerness and excitement as children of earlier centuries – the annual fair! Like the seasons of the year, the fair could be relied upon to arrive during the second week of September. Only the older children could remember the war years. Then the fair had consisted of old Mr. Smith with his single stall selling paper windmills. His presence each year had ensured the continuity of the fair and, thereby, its survival. Should the fair fail to be held on any one occasion the charter would be broken and the right to the annual fair would cease outright. Sadly, the decision taken in the late fifties to realign Adversane crossroads swiftly brought to an end a centuries old tradition. There were some who were glad to be rid of the noise, which interfered with their enjoyment of their televisions. There were others who lamented its passing, but they mourned in vain. In the age of the motor car, the fair was regarded by many as an anachronism. In the early fifties, however, the possibility of losing the fair in a few years time never entered the heads of the excited children, as they waited in eager anticipation for the arrival of the first lorries and vans.

School recommenced after the summer holidays in the first week of September. There was little enthusiasm for the new school year among the Adversane children. But, like a spark of light amid the encircling gloom of arithmetic tests and homework, was the knowledge that if the school year had started, the fair could not be far behind. As the decrepit school bus chugged over the railway crossing and into the hamlet, the older children began pushing and jostling, ignoring the swearing and shouting of the sour-faced bus driver, all striving to be first to see if the fair had arrived. When the cry, "Fair's here. It's come!" echoed down the length of the bus, there was a scramble to be first to the exit.

The children flew indoors, quickly abandoning their school bags. Within a few minutes they were congregating on the green next to the Blacksmith's Arms, chatting to the fair folk, watching the unloading of the rides and stalls and discussing what each collection of tarpaulin and poles might be transformed into.

There was one particularly spectacular year in the early fifties when two fair families combined to produce a really big funfair. There were two roundabouts, dodgems, swing boats, and a multitude of stalls, rides and entertainments. These were all erected on the far green, in time-honoured tradition, either side of the road to Wisborough Green. As the fair was assembled the familiar landmarks were blotted out. Southlands Farm and the crumbling remnants of the pound, the road itself and even the pointed eaves of Juppsland were hidden behind the densely-packed rows of stalls and large rides.

There was no room for the travelling people to set up camp round the edges of the fair as they usually did, so once the verges of the road had been covered with vans they over-flowed into a nearby field, with the willing consent of the landowner. Some of them, however, parked on the green directly in front of the old malthouse. The children were delighted, but Ethel felt shut in and over-looked, and drew the curtains early in the evening, (although she was happy to fill the women's kettles and buckets with water). Deborah knelt next to the window, the bright light of her own living-room hidden behind the drawn curtains, and with the window nets draped down her back like a wedding train, she stared unashamedly at the life outside. Everyone seemed busy and cheerful. Women hung newly-washed clothes on temporary lines, slung between the vans. Tethered dogs leapt and barked on the ends of their long ropes, attracting the attention of the untidy children, who played and rolled with them in the grass. As the light faded, mothers bathed their babies and toddlers in bowls of water just outside the vans, while older women and girls prepared the evening meals. Nights were drawing in quickly now, and the men soon left their work on the fair and came over to the vans, where they sat chatting over mugs of tea! As mellow light from the gypsies' lanterns bathed the grass in front of each home, the green became a stage and the moving figures like actors in a play. The watching child considered how much nicer life must be for those care-free children, now seated on the steps of their vans, eating a late supper by lantern-light. She could hear them playing outside long after she had gone to bed. No thought of school tomorrow for them.

  To have to go to school at this time was purgatory for the Adversane children. Their day dragged along with its usual round of tests, writing exercises and games, but at last it was time for them to board the bus back home. Here the foreign invaders had successfully and totally conquered the hamlet and made it their own. The children, at least, welcomed the invasion with all their hearts.

  For three nights the fair ran its increasingly noisy course. Antony and Deborah went every night, but only had a few pennies to spend, which they managed to add to by some skilful play on the Roll-a-penny! On Saturday evening their parents both came to the fair with them and they were given some extra pocket money, which was a rare privilege. As years went by, David spent less and less time with his family, but in the early fifties he was part of it. Holding tightly to her parents' hands, Deborah moved through the crowds, bewildered but delighted by the assault on her senses: the continuous bawling of the fair people, the regular crash and clang of the bell as the local men tried their strength, the tinny music blaring forth from the dodgems, the wonderful, precise music from the traditional merry-go-round. The air was heavy with a smell of fried onions and boiled sugar, mingling with oil and crushed grass. She ate candyfloss and a toffee apple, increasingly sticky and increasingly happy! David won a coconut, Ethel proved to be exceptionally gifted on the Roll-a-penny and Antony won a china cruet by rolling balls to get a winning score. Deborah fished for a surprise bag and found a little plastic animal inside it. She wanted a little goldfish to carry home in a bag, but Ethel would not hear of them even trying. "It's not fair unless you have a proper tank," she said firmly.

Deborah had two rides on the small roundabout, saving the enormous merry-go-round till last. The family had kept going back to it throughout the evening - mesmerized by the whirling lights, cantering ponies, prancing ostriches and fantastic dragon-shaped boats. The little figures in the centre piped and drummed as the music spilled out in a continuous flow of musical notes. As the time to leave the fair came closer, they went back once again to the merry-go-round, which dominated the centre of the fair. Deborah found herself being lifted up by her father, as the roundabout slowed once more. She was seated in front of him on a magnificent, two-saddled galloper. Reverently she stroked its flowing mane, patted its shiny cheek, while David handed their money over to the lean man whom she had seen deftly jumping inbetween the animals, collecting the fares. Now they were gathering up speed. The horse rose and fell, rose and fell, faster and faster. In spite of her father's arms around her, Deborah clung to the twisted pole with all her might, not liking to let go even for a moment to wave to her mother, who was standing way below, smiling and waving at them. On the adjacent horse her brother grinned and shouted at her as they whirled and whirled round, his voice lost in the clatter of the music. Deborah saw the illuminated horse-shoe shaped sign of the Blacksmith's Arms flash past, the dark and sombre trees screening Juppsland's garden, a shadowy line of caravans stretching away down the Newbridge road. Then she saw the fair, the main road and the row of cottages where they lived, then back to the inn sign again. Looking up, the moon and stars were almost non-existent, eclipsed by the brilliance of the multi-coloured lights shining out around the fairground. The roundabout was slowing again and the blurred images began to look clearer. It was safe to take one hand away and wave at her mother. Sadly she waited for her father to lift her off the horse.... but they were having another ride! It was too good to be true, but they were galloping away again, into the lights, the night sky, the dark fields, the crowded fair, while the little band kept drumming and clashing for all it was worth!

****

Adversane had its own, thriving bonfire society, keeping up with the local villages, in spite of its small size. Around the 5th November bonfires crackled and roared and fireworks banged and cascaded in a different village each evening, with local societies attending each other's events to add support and colour and to maximize the celebrations!

Billingshurst had a bigger bonfire, of course, and hosted the 5th November event, but Adversane put on a good show. There were fancy dress contests for adults and children, who paraded in the Mission Hall for judging before the fireworks began. After the bonfire and fireworks there was a dance in the hall for the grown-ups.

When Deborah was five she entered the fancy dress contest for the first time. She wore a dark blue dress covered in silver stars and "fireworks", made from card and paper. David painted the words "Adversane Bonfire Society" onto a suitably decorated placard to hang on her back. Deborah thought this a rather dull costume until she saw the head-dress, made by Auntie Flip's clever fingers. It was a bonfire, constructed from tiny twigs, topped by a perfect Guy Fawkes, complete with a bristling beard, velvet suit and stove-pipe hat, with a tiny feather in the band.

Antony was dressed as a pirate and built up to the part throughout the day, waving a toy cutlass aloft and singing,

"Fifteen men on a dead man's chest,
Yo, ho, ho and a bottle of rum...",
rolling the r's in rum for dramatic effect. Deborah joyfully joined in, "Drink and the devil had done for the rest,
Yo, ho, ho and a bottle of rum!"

They kept the chorus up until Ethel's patience snapped and she told them to stop making that awful noise.

When at last evening came the atmosphere was electric! The children were in an agony of excitement, dressed in their costumes. The reverberating boom, boom of a bass drum sent them running to peer out of the window, as the West Chiltington band marched past the Blacksmith's Arms to the procession assembly point.

Their father burst in from outdoors, as excited as they were. He was looking very dashing, dressed in Regency style with a wig, breeches and long jacket. He was on the society committee and was acting as Master of Ceremonies at the Bonfire Dance later on that evening.

"Time for the fancy dress competition," he called, sticking his head round the side of the door. "Are you ready?"

"Nearly," shouted Ethel, struggling into her coat. "You should see May," David laughed. "She says she's Annie Bawlin!"

"She's who?"

"Annie Bawlin – you know. One of Henry VIII's wives!"

Everyone laughed at the joke, including Deborah, who didn't understand it.

They were, at last, ready. Ethel was satisfied that the fire was safe to leave, the back door firmly secured, the wireless at a sufficiently loud volume to soothe the dog's nerves when the fireworks started and the cat safely tucked away under the range. She locked the front door and, as she always did, tried the handle several times before being satisfied it was well locked.

Outside the brightly lit cosiness of the living-room there was a very different world. The frosty night air was vibrant: the atmosphere charged with excitement and drenched with the smell of paraffin. Strangers approached from familiar doorways, all moving towards the yellow lights winking from the windows of the Mission

Hall, only they turned out not to be strangers after all! The golliwog was Deborah's friend, Thelma, and the frightening spectral figure next to her was her brother, Len. The policeman directing them towards the hall was Mr. Frank from the shop and the beautiful lady in a long dress and tall hat, (like the one riding to Banbury Cross in Deborah's nursery rhyme book), was not really Annie Bawlin but her beloved neighbour, Mrs. Ahern!

David went ahead, to attend to his official duties. The rest of the family joined the queue of people filing in through the narrow door. There was a short delay when Audrey Gregory got stuck trying to get her costume through. She was dressed as a roundabout, with little animals and toys suspended from a wooden hoop all around her. A group of admiring adults tried to ease her through the door without losing any of the pieces.

Deborah craned her neck past the roundabout and saw her father coming towards her, looking so dashing in the blue satin breeches and lacy cravat. Her heart swelled with pride, but her emotions quickly changed to jealousy when he finally managed to get Audrey through the door and complimented her on her costume! Ethel could read her daughter like a book, and gave her a ticking off for being so silly. Deborah felt small, until her father picked her up and danced off with her to the tinny tones of a waltz coming from the gramophone. He set her back on the ground, where her parents began attaching her Adversane Bonfire Society placard to her back. So many people were squeezing into the hall, parents ushering their children into line in readiness for the judging. While Deborah gazed admiringly at a boy dressed as her great hero – Rupert Bear – her own name was called. She had won a prize!

After the prizes were handed out, coats were put on top of costumes and people began to pour out of the hall to join the torchlight procession which, headed by the band, was making its way to the bonfire field. Here the black hulk of an enormous bonfire was just discernible through the gloom. Torches bobbed in the darkness, as men made ready to set it alight.

"There's the Guy," Antony pointed out.

Deborah could see the small figure on top of the mountain in front of them. She knew it was just a straw figure wearing a mask, but she also knew people really had been burned to death in the past, and once the flames flared up her anguish increased for the tiny crooked figure awaiting his fate at the top of the pyre. As the heat intensified the crowd moved back and Guy suddenly toppled and fell down the side of the burning heap to cries of delight from the spectators. Deborah, already unnerved by the Jumping Jacks which were being tossed into the crowd by some of the youths, began to cry. Her mother led her to the roadside, where they watched the rockets, Roman Candles and Catherine Wheels from a safe distance.

Once the fireworks were over and the bonfire reduced to half its size, people began to move back into the Mission Hall, where there were sausage rolls, bags of crisps and toffee apples, (the best of which, Deborah was quite sure, were those her mother had made!)

The time came for the children to go home. Ethel saw them into their beds before returning to the Bonfire Dance and her dashing M.C. There were few opportunities for Ethel and David to dance now and it brought back happy memories of her years in Cricklewood and the dancing competitions.

At home Deborah knelt on her bed and peered through the curtains at the glowing embers of the bonfire. The smell of smoke and sulphur crept in through the ill-fitting frame, together with a steady blast of cold night air. She got into bed and pulled the blankets over her head to muffle the sound of Victor Silvester, which resonated through the night from the hall. There were regular bangs, screams and shouts which continued into the early hours, long after she heard the thud of the front door closing, which told her that her parents had returned and the family was complete.

****

Soon after Bonfire Night came the Sunday School Christmas Party. Deborah was not a lover of parties, apart from Mrs. Baxter's, which were in a class of their own. She knew everyone there, which helped. But Sunday School parties were shared with the

Antony & Deborah's bonfire fancy dress 1952

Billingshurst Sunday School and there were a lot of unfamiliar faces. They were held alternately in the Women's Hall one year, the Adversane Mission Hall the next. The Billingshurst children travelled down to Adversane on the local bus when it was the hamlet's turn to host the party. Sunday School teachers and helpers conducted the untidy crocodile of excited children the short distance from the bus stop to the Mission Hall. The hall was looking its best, generously festooned with paper chains and balloons, and with a small Christmas tree on the cribbage table in one corner. The Adversane Sunday School was outnumbered by this cheerful invasion and the local children stood self-consciously in one corner, watching their noisy neighbours discarding their coats and gloves. The girls from both village and hamlet wore their best party dresses, with a cardigan on top (which was soon left on a chair, so they could show their dresses off to the best advantage). Even the shortest hair was embellished with ribbons and slides.

  Down the centre of the hall was a long table, covered with plates of paste and cheese sandwiches, assorted cakes and – in the middle – a large pink, blancmange rabbit. A small boy began racing up and down in the confined space, ignoring the requests of the Billingshurst helpers to blow his nose. A piece of rag was pinned to his shirt for this purpose, but he preferred to let it run! He was too busy leaning across the cakes and poking a finger into the rabbit blancmange! After tea, (Deborah skipped the blancmange), the tables were swiftly cleared and space made for games. These were the traditional ever-popular ones – Pass the Parcel, Squeak Piggy Squeak, Pin the Tail on the Donkey, Musical Chairs, Statues and Oranges and Lemons. That was a great favourite, but nearly everyone wanted to be on the side of the oranges so they always won the tug of war at the end.

  The high-light of these parties came at the end of the afternoon. Experienced party-goers looked for the first signs – adults whispering secretively together and looking expectantly at one another. The children were told to sit in the chairs around the walls.

  "Can you hear someone coming?" asked the Vicar's wife. I

can hear sleigh bells!" Mrs. Farquharson jovially remarked.

There followed a rapid knocking on the door. The older children looked knowingly at one another while the little ones turned rather anxiously in their chairs and studied the faces around them. Was it a nice or a nasty surprise?

The door was flung wide to admit Father Christmas and his sack of presents.

Every child received a gift. As names were called they went up to receive a parcel and were invited to thank Father Christmas with a kiss. When it was Deborah's turn she peered into the face bent over hers. She was not fooled by the disguise, and would not get any closer to those false whiskers behind which she knew lurked the rather cross features of Bill Etherington from Hadfold! She was a little worried she might not get her present if she refused, but it was worth the risk. Luckily her reluctance was put down to shyness and she got the parcel, which contained a beautiful fairy doll, with blonde hair and a tinsel wand.

When all the presents had been given out a wail went up from one small boy who had not received anything from Santa's sack. The children watched, eyes round with concern, as adults tried to comfort him. One of the older Billingshurst girls had a quick consultation with a helper and handed the boy her present. His sobs ceased instantly, and a sigh of relief swept round the room. The girl pressed her lips together but kept a dry eye. Perhaps she had a reward later. The children's parents bought and wrapped the presents, which were taken to the hall and put in the sack. The boy who had not received anything presumably came from a family who could not afford one, or could not be bothered. Either way, he was quickly soothed and went home happy.

Deborah in Coronation costume 1953

Epilogue

So the seasons came and the seasons went and the years rolled away through the fifties, revealing little obvious change in the life of the small community of Adversane. Yet the changes were there, although so slight and subtle no-one really noticed them. By the middle of the decade more and more families had a television set in one corner of the sitting-room; presiding over their lives, revered and cherished like a religious icon. Numbers dropped away at the film nights, socials and whist drives as people settled in to watch the magic box, so these events were eventually dropped.

The two double-decker buses which transported people to work and school and back each day were reduced to one, as car ownership began to take off and passenger numbers fell. Traffic grew busier, especially at weekends. But it was still a quiet and insular place most of the time, and remained very much a country hamlet. The sound of sheep bleating and cows lowing was far more familiar than the roar of car engines, and the appearance of the hamlet changed little.

As Deborah approached her tenth birthday, ("double figures", her grandmother had pointed out, emphasizing the milestone), she became increasingly conscious of how beautiful the countryside around her was, and how powerfully it held her. From her earliest years she had always been aware that almost every cottage, house and farm in the surrounding area, had at some time or another been home to an Evershed, a Taylor, a Puttock or a Humphrey!

When she and her brother walked down Westlands Lane they passed a field, full of hummocks and hillocks, which marked the site of the cottage where her paternal grandparents had raised four of their five children. In that lane her Aunt Joan had snatched a toddling Uncle Bert from the path of a rampaging carthorse, saving him from being trampled underfoot. Further along, on the right, there was a cottage where her great-uncle and aunt had raised their four boys, and beyond that was the half-timbered Soil Farm, where her great-great-great-great Uncle Hezekiah and Aunt Mary had farmed a hundred years ago.

The path they trod through the woods had been a familiar trackway for her grandfather Eldred, as he regularly drove his horse and cart past Lee Place to Wisborough Green, and had been the route he took one April night to fetch the doctor to attend his wife in childbirth. If they walked past the entrance to the woods they could glimpse the chimneys of the ancient farm, Nobs Crook, familiar to them as the subject of a painting by their great-grandfather, David Wood. It had also been the home of their great-great-grandparents!

When the children took the lane east from Lee Place they came to Haybourne, where their maternal grandmother had lived as a little girl – a place of old hedgerows resonant with the sound of humming insects, laden with blackberries in late summer and always rustling with the busy sound of hedge sparrows.

Walking to Kingslea from Adversane was a similar experience! Tom Taylor had lived in the 1898 house, maternal great-grandparents in one of the cottages on the right approaching Beke, then further along that road Uncle Bert and Aunt Gladys, and then there was Beke Lodge, where Antony had been born.

It seemed right and proper to the young girl that she should be walking in her ancestors' footprints, and she never tired of learning about them from her parents, her grandmother and aunts.

Playing outside in the long spring or summer evenings, Deborah never really felt quite alone! One evening in May, as other children left the green and went indoors, she lingered behind. Her favourite spot was next to Coe's barn, where the setting sun struck a deeper gold into the yellow of the buttercups. Birds twittered incessantly in the hedges of Griggs' cottages as they sensed the coming of night, but swallows continued to swoop across the hamlet in the fading light. Standing next to the ancient barn, Deborah looked across at the old malthouse, brooding peacefully in the evening sunshine. On the other side of the deserted road lights began to shine from the shadowy interior of the Blacksmith's Arms. But golden sunlight still slanted down the garden fronting Juppsland, lighting up the the creamy blossom of the tall hawthorns which grew at the corner of Westlands Lane.

Deborah's gaze moved back to the inn, then left towards the snug little forge, tucked away in the shadow of encircling ash trees. Next to the forge was "Sayers", standing silently on its own, with only an occasional ripple from its pond to indicate occupation of any kind, for the house itself was empty! There was a "For Sale" board outside the neat white fence. The windows were dark and the garden was rapidly falling into shadow. It seemed to the child that the house knew who she was and it needed her to come and take away its loneliness. Deborah quickly crossed the road, pushed open the gate and walked down the path at the side with confidence. Standing by the back door she gazed at the long garden, taking it all in, savouring the moment. It was still sunny and warm here. She sensed a friendly and joyous welcome and felt it had not just been the house which had called her. It was something, or somebody, else. Deborah pressed her nose against the kitchen window and peered inside. It all looked just as she knew it would. Everything was as it should be.

"Who ever buys it," she thought, "I know a little part of it will always belong to me, because I am part of Grandmother Deborah!"

With reluctance she walked lingeringly back along the path, knowing she would not visit there again. She closed the gate, crossed the road and went back across the green, where bats had taken over the sky from the swallows. Her mother would be wondering where she was. She paused a moment, holding the front door open and looking back at "Sayers", resting quietly in the twilight. A rustle above her head reminded her that the swallows had settled down for the night in their nests above the porch. Very gently she closed the door and felt her way along the line of coats in the dark hallway, seeking the door to the living-room, where she could hear the wireless and her father's ringing laughter.

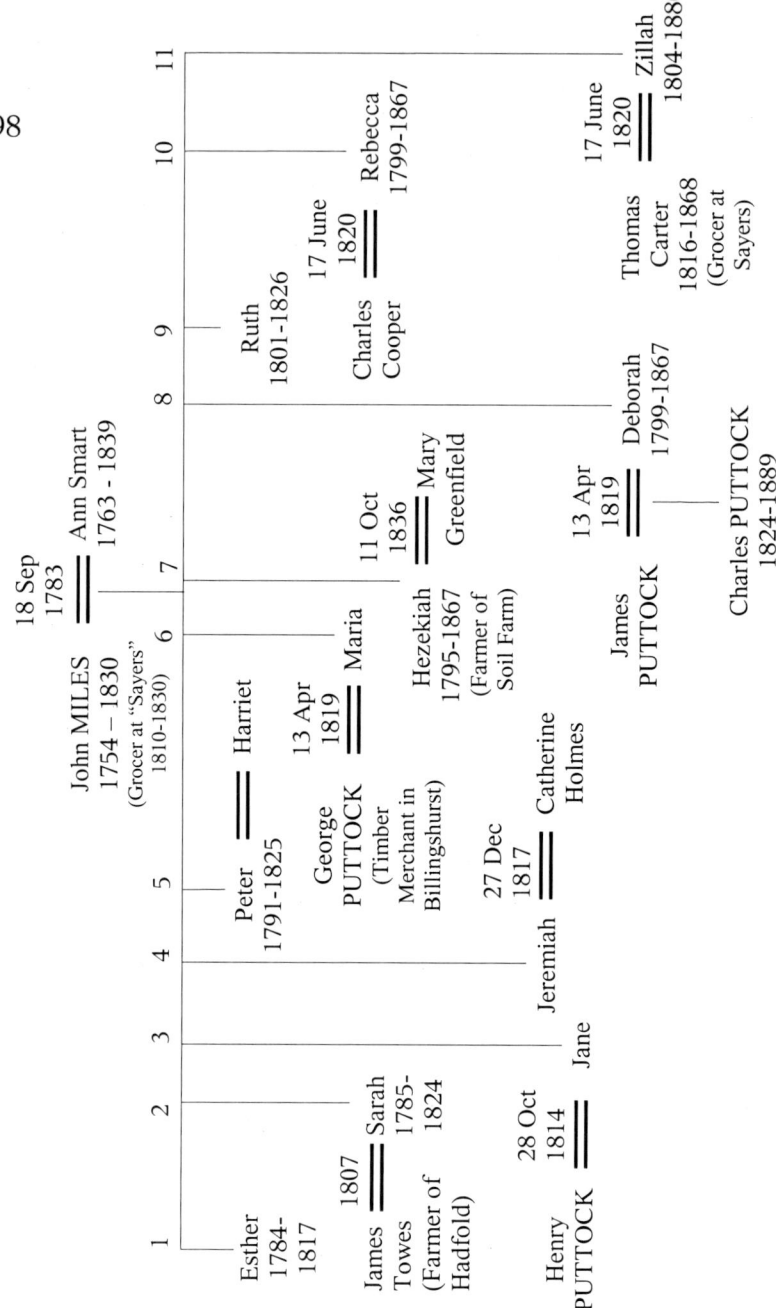

Part of Miles family tree

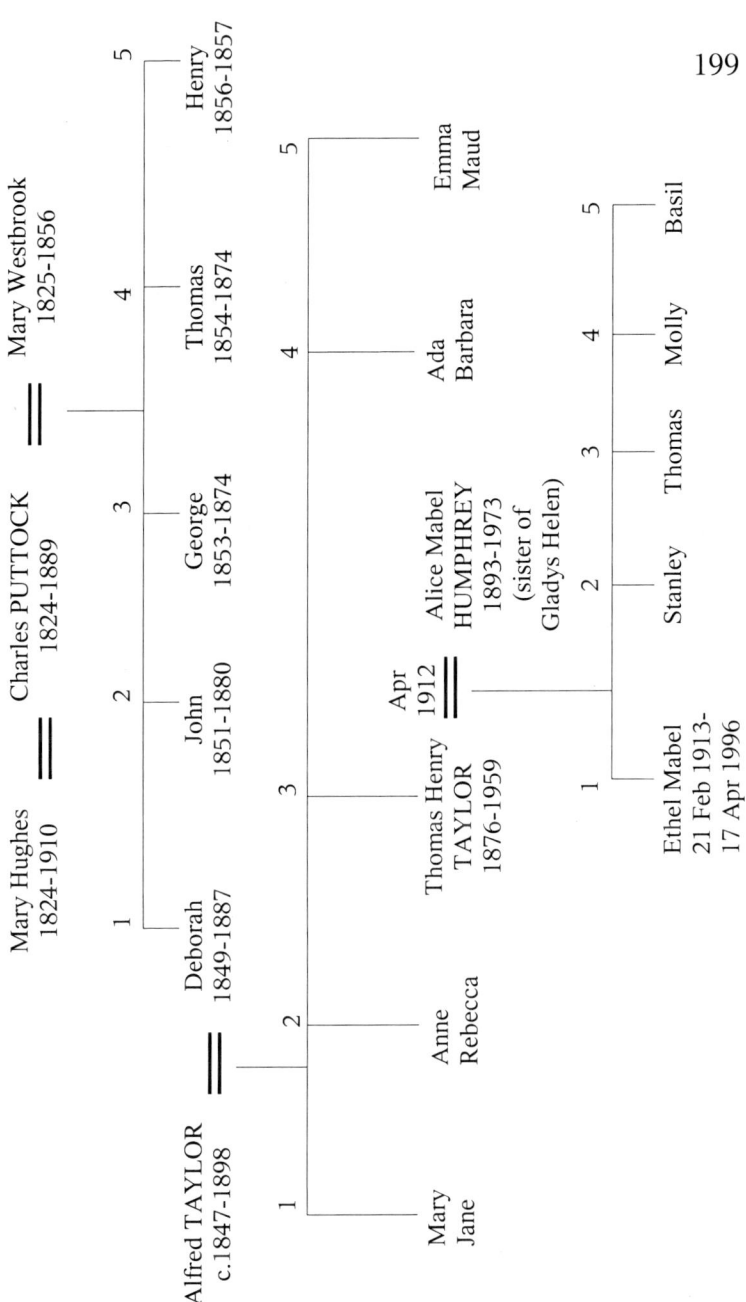

Part of Puttock & Taylor family trees

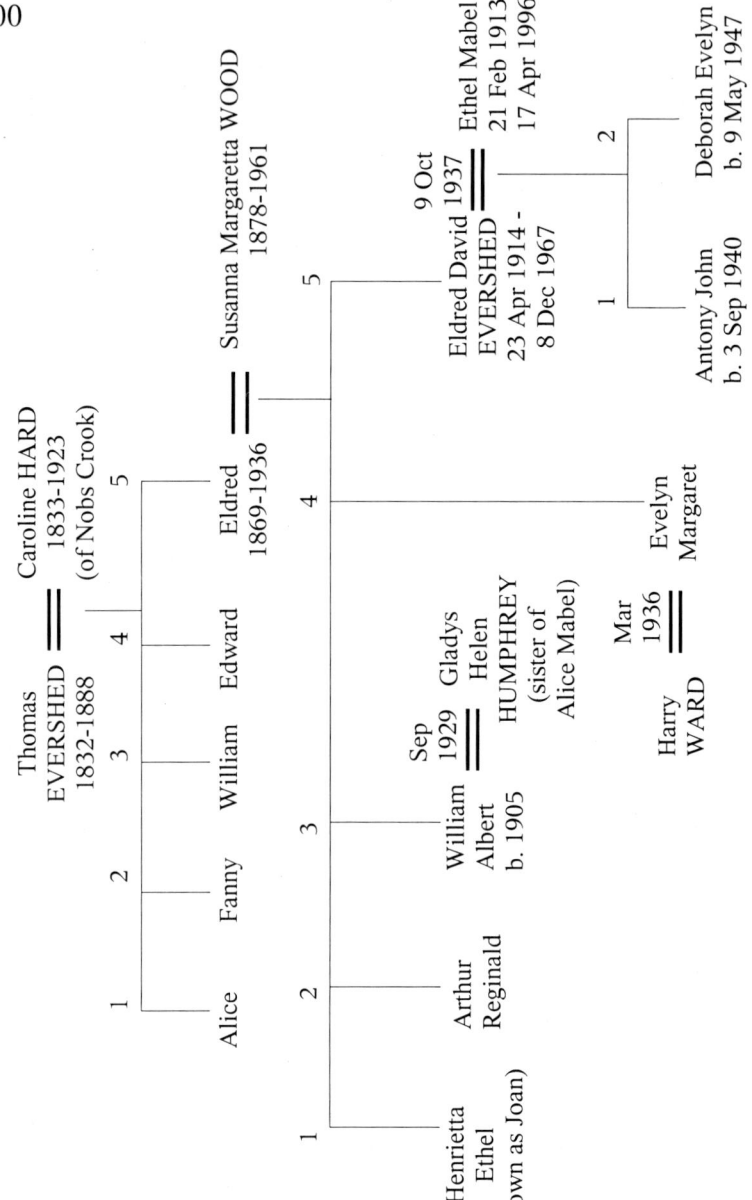

Part of Evershed family tree